Baking Is Fun

Volume 1

ISBN 0-9691357-0-X

Printed and Bound in Austria

European baking, cakes and tortes in particular are world renowned for their beauty and quality. We have put together for you a selection of our favourites.

A wide range of Oetker's baking ingredients are packaged individually in premeasured amounts suited to all your baking needs. This minimizes risk of error in measuring and ensures that optimum quality is maintained.

The recipes in this cookbook have been developed and tested to help you take full advantage of the accuracy and convenience of Oetker products so that you can duplicate the European specialties in your own home with ease and confidence.

Happy Baking in the European tradition!

Yours sincerely
OETKER Recipe Service

Contents

Baking Tips

Recipes

1. Brush pan generously with shortening or spray with recommended vegetable coating spray. Be sure to get into all corners and folds. Add a little flour to the pan and shake pan to spread flour evenly until it covers the surface. Shake out excess flour. It is advisable to prepare teflon pans the same way.

2. Waxed Paper Lined Pans
To line a straight-sided square or rectangular pan neatly with waxed paper, set pan on paper. Trace outline of pan base. Tilt pan to all 4 sides drawing outline of each side on the paper. Cut out outline. You should have a base with 4 sides attached and the corners cut out. Fold up sides. Grease a few spots on pan so paper will stick. Fit paper into pan.

3. Pans for Sponge Cakes
Grease bottom only, NOT sides, of spring form pan. Trace outline of pan onto waxed paper. Cut out and fit paper round into bottom of pan.

Filling:

1. To cut cake in even layers: Place cake, smooth side up, on board. Decide what thickness you want the layers cut, then insert toothpicks all around the cake about 2 cm (1″) apart.
Under toothpicks, cut all around cake about .5 cm (1/4″) in from edge. Using a strong thread, place it into the cut all around the cake. Pull thread tightly to cut through cake.

2. Instead of thread you can cut cake with knife which is longer than the cake diameter. Mark place with toothpicks as above. Slice through cake with knife using a sawing motion.

3. Lift layer(s) of cake off with a cake spatula to prepare cake for filling.

4. Spread filling on cake layers with cake spreader or spatula.

5. To make an even layer cake, fill bottom cake layer as desired. Using cake lifter or spatula place second cake layer over filling. Press down lightly and move if necessary to make sure the edges of the cake layers line up evenly. Repeat with number of fillings and cake layers desired.

Glazing & Decorating:

1. Place cake on waxed paper. Spread your filling or frosting on top of cake to cover completely. For a smooth, even surface with a long spatula or knife go over cake from right to left without lifting spatula.

2. For even distribution of frosting, spread frosting with a spatula around sides of cake, start from middle and work in an upwards motion. For a smooth even top, dip spatula into lukewarm water and smooth over cake lightly.

3. To decorate sides of cake with chopped nuts, sliced almonds, toasted coconut, grated chocolate or chocolate sprinkles, spread a thin layer of frosting over cake. Cover sides generously with desired decoration by pushing it upwards from bottom and pressing into frosting lightly.

4. To decorate with decorating bag:
Use desired frosting suitable for decorating such as whipped cream, meringue, OETKER Frosting Mix or buttercream frosting (cool). Attach desired nozzle to bag as directed. Fill bag with frosting. DO NOT overfill. It is much easier to work with a bag that is not too full. Twist top of bag closed as you would turn a screw. Hold filled bag on top of filling and at bottom so your hand won't be holding where filling is. The heat of your hand can melt the filling.

5. To lift cake off waxed paper and onto cake plate:
Place spatula under cake. Lift spatula with one hand and place other hand under cake. Lift carefully and place onto plate.

To Glaze:
1. Place cake on waxed paper. If you brush cake lightly with a jam such as apricot your glaze will spread better, smoother and more evenly. For best results, heat jam slightly and strain through a sieve.

2. Pour slightly warmed glaze onto centre of cake.

3. Let glaze run down sides of cake until cake is completely covered.

4. Holding spatula or knife on an angle, use glaze that has run off cake onto paper at bottom edge and spread smoothly onto sides of cake by using an upward motion.

5. To avoid cracks in glaze place cake on cake plate while glaze is still soft OR wait until glaze is completely dry to move it.

TO GARNISH with nuts, candied fruit, streusel, etc., quickly place garnish on cake while glaze is still soft and wet. If glaze is dry the garnish will not stick and will fall off.

Cream butter or margarine until creamy. Gradually add sugar, OETKER Vanilla Sugar, eggs, OETKER Essences, spices and salt, beating until light and fluffy. Sift flour and OETKER Baking Powder together. Add to creamed mixture alternately with milk, using just enough milk to make a batter that falls from a spoon in large pieces. If using dried fruits or nuts in your recipe fold into batter at the end. Turn batter into greased and floured pans.

Break Down:

1. If creaming batter by hand, the butter or margarine will work best if it is soft. Place butter or margarine in mixing bowl and beat with wooden spoon until creamy. Creaming can also be done easily with an electric mixer.

2. Gradually add sugar and OETKER Vanilla Sugar to creamed butter, beating until sugar no longer feels grainy. For best results use fine granulated or fruit sugar. Use icing sugar if stated in recipe. Coarse sugar is dissolved very slowly and could affect rising of cake.

3. Have eggs at room temperature. Break each egg into a cup to ensure against adding a bad one then add one at a time to creamed mixture, beating well after each. Eggs also help to dissolve any undissolved sugar in creamed mixture.

4. Add OETKER Essence, salt (if unsalted butter is used) and spices to creamed mixture. Stir well to blend.

5. Sift flour and OETKER Baking Powder together. Add to creamed mixture alternately with liquid, combining lightly after each addition. Sifting the flour and baking powder together will make a finer, even-textured, lighter cake. Combine ingredients lightly after each addition because if baking powder comes in direct contact with the liquid it starts working immediately and thus loses some of its leavening power before baking.

6. Just add enough milk so that mixture is slightly heavy and falls off a spoon in blobs. The amount of milk will depend on the size of eggs and the absorbency of the other ingredients. That's why in creamed batters an exact amount of milk cannot be given. There is usually a range in the amount of milk. The batter has the right consistency when it falls off the spoon in heavy blobs. There is one exception where the batter should run off the spoon. This is a batter that is high in butter and eggs and lower in dry ingredients.

7. Fold dried fruits or nuts into batter at the end. eg. raisins, currants, candied fruits, chopped nuts, chocolate chips, etc. Fold carefully so batter does not get grey looking or is over beaten.

8. Preheat oven to desired temperature. Turn batter into prepared pan which has been greased and lightly floured or as directed in recipe. Level top of batter with a cake spreader or spatula. Fill pan only ⅔ full. If there is too much batter in the pan cake will not rise properly and could overflow.

To test for doneness, insert a toothpick in centre of cake. If it comes out clean the cake is done. If cake sticks to the toothpick bake 5 min longer and test again.

Cool cake in pan 5-10 min, no longer. Turn out on wire rack to cool completely.

Sift flour and OETKER Baking Powder together onto pastry board or flat surface. Make a well in the centre. Put sugar, OETKER Vanilla Sugar, salt if using unsalted butter, OETKER Essence, spices, eggs and liquid if required (milk or water) into well. Work a little flour into centre ingredients to make a thick paste. Cut cold butter or margarine into small pieces over centre ingredients on board. Cover with some of the flour and quickly work all ingredients together into a soft, smooth dough. Form dough into a ball. Wrap well and store in a cool place until ready to use.

Break Down:

1. Sift flour and OETKER Baking Powder onto pastry board or flat surface. Make a well in the centre. Sifting the flour and OETKER Baking Powder together mixes the two ingredients evenly. Sifting will make a finer textured dough which is also flakier. If recipe calls for cocoa or chocolate powder it should be sifted with the flour.

2. Put sugar, OETKER Vanilla Sugar, salt if using unsalted butter, OETKER Essence, spices, eggs and liquid if required (milk or water) into well. Always break egg into a cup to check for freshness before adding to other ingredients.

3. Mix a little flour into centre ingredients with a fork to make a thick paste. By mixing in just a small amount of flour first it will be easier to work in the remaining flour.

4. Cut cold butter into small pieces over centre ingredients. Always use cold butter or margarine. This gives a dough that is easy to knead. If butter is hot the dough will be sticky and difficult to work with. Put a little flour over the butter. This keeps the butter from sticking to your hands and dough will be easier to work with.

5. Quickly work all ingredients together into a soft, smooth dough.
Kneading the dough consists of 3 steps:

a) Place both hands under the dough and fold upper half over lower half. Do not hold dough too long in your hands or it will become too soft from the warmth of your hands.

b) Press dough down lightly with the heel of your hands. Keep hands floured so dough will not get sticky.

c) Turning – place heel of hands on dough. Lightly turn and press ¼ turn to the right. This way you will pick up the flour still on the board. Continue turning and pressing, scrape board occasionally to loosen flour towards dough so that all the flour will be picked up by the dough.

6. Shape dough into a roll or ball. The roll is best if dough is to be rolled out to a rectangular shape and the ball is best for dough that is to be rolled into a round. If dough sticks to board, chill slightly. This dough is rich in butter and softens if it is warm. DO NOT add more flour or your dough will become crumbly and tough. In doughs that have liquid in the ingredients you can add a little more flour to keep it from sticking. Dough is easier to roll out if it is cold. You can make it a day ahead of time if desired. Wrap well and store in refrigerator. Soften at room temperature just until easy to roll.

Puff Pastry

Basic Recipe:
The preparation of puff pastry is time consuming but it can be used in a wide variety of recipes, such as cream slices, tarts, sausage rolls, etc. Puff pastry keeps several days in the refrigerator and it can also be frozen. Thus you may prefer to double or triple the basic recipe since the working time is the same as for a single amount. Puff Pastry Working Method is repeated 5 times. In between each time the dough has to rest in a COOL place.

250 mL	butter or margarine, softened	1 cup
800 mL	all-purpose flour	3¼ cups
175 mL	ice water	¾ cup
250 mL	cold butter or margarine	1 cup

Method:
Cut softened butter into small pieces. Work into flour with fingers. Make a well in the centre. Put water into well. Work all ingredients together to form a soft, smooth dough. Roll out dough to a rectangle 1 cm (½″) thick. Cut cold butter into small pieces and distribute evenly over dough (see picture). Fold narrow sides of dough into centre. Roll out to a rectangle again. Butter will mix with dough in the rolling. Fold again then wrap and chill 30 min. Repeat rolling, folding and 30 min chilling 4 to 5 times. Before rolling the folded dough turn it ¼ turn to the right.
MAKES about 1kg (2 lbs.) puff pastry dough

Break Down:
1. Cut softened butter or margarine into pieces. Work into flour with fingers. Make a well in centre. Add ice water. Work all ingredients together to form a soft, smooth dough.

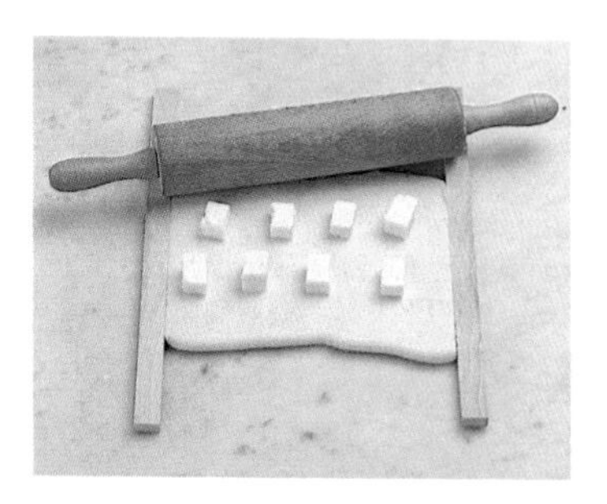

2. Roll out dough to a rectangle 1 cm (½″) thick. Two wooden sticks have been used in picture for measuring thickness. The dough should be evenly thick. Cut cold butter into small pieces and distribute evenly over dough.

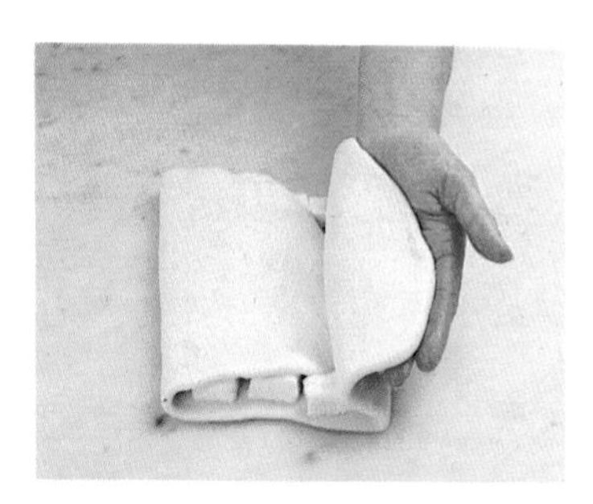

3. Fold narrow sides of dough into centre (like folding a towel). Roll out to a rectangle again. Butter will mix with dough in the rolling. Fold again then wrap and refrigerate 30 min. This is working method no. 1

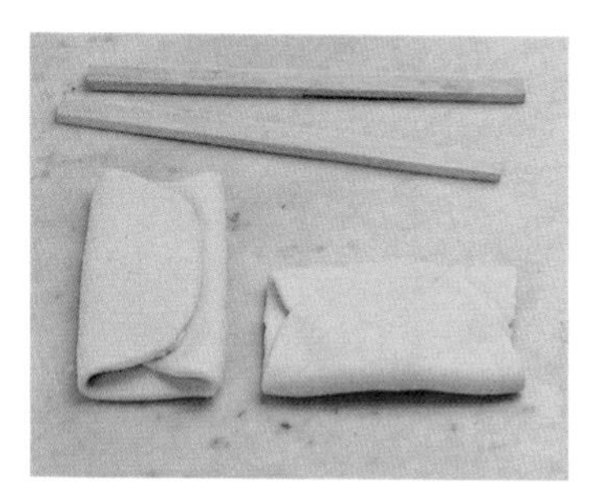

4. Repeat the same working method of rolling, folding and 30 min chilling 4 to 5 times.
Before each rolling out of the folded dough, turn dough ¼ turn to the right so it is rolled once from the folded side and the next time from the open side. This repeated rolling and folding is what gives you the "layers of puff."
Use a sharp knife to cut puff pastry dough. Do not use egg yolk or milk to seal seams or ends together or dough will not rise evenly.
Chill baking sheet before putting puff pastry on it to minimize shrinkage during baking.

Sponge Cake

6	egg yolks	6
175 mL	sugar	¼ cup
2 pkg.	OETKER Vanilla Sugar	2 pkg.
30 mL	hot water	2 tbsp.
5–6 drops	OETKER Lemon Essence	5–6 drops
6	egg whites	6
250 mL	all-purpose flour	1 cup
5 mL	OETKER Baking Powder	1 tsp.

Beat egg yolks and water on high speed of electric mixer until creamy. Gradually add ⅔ of sugar and OETKER Vanilla Sugar beating until thick and creamy. Add OETKER Essence and spices. Beat egg whites, gradually adding remaining sugar until stiff peaks form.
Turn stiffly beaten egg whites over creamy egg yolk mixture. Sift flour and OETKER Baking Powder together over egg whites. Fold all ingredients gently but thoroughly.
Turn batter into greased and waxed paper lined pan.

Break Down:
1. Break 1 egg into a cup. Separate yolk from white. Repeat with remaining eggs keeping all yolks in one bowl and all whites in a metal or glass bowl (not plastic).
Beat yolks and water together with electric mixer or whisk until foamy and creamy. This should take about 3 min with electric mixer or 15 min with a whisk. The amount of water will depend on the size of eggs used.

Sponge Cake

2. Gradually add ⅔ of sugar and OETKER Vanilla Sugar, beating until thick and creamy. Add sugar 15 mL (1 tbsp.) at a time to ensure a thick mixture with no grains of sugar in it. To test consistency let some of the mixture run off your whisk or beaters. If the drops stay on top of mixture in the bowl before blending in, the consistency is right. Now add OETKER Essence and spices.

3. Be sure your bowl and beaters or whisk are free from grease or whites will not beat. Beat egg whites to soft peaks. Gradually add the remaining sugar 15 mL (1 tbsp.) at a time, beating until stiff peaks form. When some of the mixture is lifted on your whisk it should hang in soft peaks. To be sure, cut through whites with a knife. If cut remains visible the consistency is right. By hand with a whisk beating will take 15-20 min. With an electric mixer start on low and when whites start to thicken turn to high. Beating will take 2-3 min.

4. Turn egg whites onto yolk mixture. Sift flour and OETKER Baking Powder and starch together over egg whites. Starch is a very fine powder that will make your cake light and airy. For chocolate sponge cake add cocoa or chocolate powder to flour mixture. Add ground nuts last, over the flour.

5. DO NOT STIR ingredients together or your egg whites will turn liquid and your cake will not rise. Use a whisk or spatula and GENTLY fold mixture working from sides of the bowl until dry ingredients are blended. This should be done QUICKLY so that the egg whites do not liquify.

6. Turn batter into a greased pan that has been lined with waxed paper. Spread batter evenly in pan. Bang pan bottom on counter to release large air bubbles. This makes a fine, even-textured cake. Bake cake immediately. To test for doneness, insert a toothpick in centre of cake. If it comes out clean the cake is done. If cake sticks to the toothpick, bake 5 min longer and test again. Also, if you touch the top of the cake in the centre gently and cake springs back, it is done. If indentation of your fingers stays in cake, bake longer.
Cool cake in pan for 10-15 min. With a pointed knife, loosen around sides of pan and remove cake from pan.
Remove waxed paper from bottom of cake. If waxed paper sticks, hold a wet cloth on the paper for a few minutes and it should come off easily. Cool cake completely on wire rack. If you want to store the cake, leave waxed paper on. Wrap in foil. Place in a plastic bag and keep in refrigerator for a few days or freeze.

Chou Pastry — for eclairs, cream puffs, etc.

Place water and butter (margarine or shortening) in saucepan. Bring to a boil.
Add flour all at once, stirring vigorously, until mixture forms a smooth ball and leaves sides of the pan. Cook stirring constantly 1 min. Turn into mixing bowl. Cool slightly.
Add eggs, 1 at a time, beating well after each addition until smooth and shiny. Cool. If recipe calls for OETKER Baking Powder, add to cooled mixture and beat well.

Break Down:

1. Place water and butter (margarine or shortening) in saucepan. Bring to a boil. Add flour all at once, stirring constantly.

2. Stir vigorously until mixture forms a smooth ball and leaves sides of pan.

3. Once ball is formed, cook stirring constantly for 1 min to dry mixture out slightly.

4. Turn mixture into a mixing bowl. Cool slightly. Add eggs, 1 at a time, beating well after each addition until smooth and shiny. It is wise to break each egg into a cup before adding to batter just in case you find a bad egg. Add only enough egg (number will depend on size) to make a batter that is shiny, smooth and tears off a spoon.

5. If recipe calls for OETKER Baking Powder, add it to cooled mixture and beat well. DO NOT add baking powder while batter is still warm as it loses its leavening power.

Yeast is a natural active rising product that has been used for hundreds of years to make breads and cakes. Yeast leavens dough by producing carbon dioxide gas which makes the dough rise. Yeast leavened products have a distinct flavour that is unique to yeast doughs. Fresh or cake yeast comes in pressed cubes and keeps about 3 weeks refrigerated. OETKER DRY YEAST keeps for months without deterioration of quality and does not have to be refrigerated.
Fresh cake yeast is dissolved in a little sugar and lukewarm water before mixing with remaining ingredients.
Dry yeast comes in two different forms. (Directions for use are on the package.)

1) Dissolve 5 mL (1 tsp.) sugar in 125 mL (½ cup) of lukewarm water or milk from recipe. Sprinkle yeast over water. Let stand 10 min then stir well. This mixture, called pre-dough, is then worked into remaining ingredients according to recipe.
2) The second type of yeast is added directly to the dry ingredients (flour, sugar, salt) according to the recipe, thus eliminating the softening in water step.

All other ingredients in the recipe, such as butter, liquid, eggs, etc., should be at room temperature.
Add only half the flour first to the other ingredients. Beat very well until dough is smooth and slightly elastic. The remaining flour is worked into the dough by kneading. Knead yeast dough until it is shiny and blistered in appearance. Shape dough into a ball. Place in a greased bowl, turning to grease top of dough. Cover with a cloth. Let dough rise in a warm place until doubled in size. Punch dough down; shape as directed. Brush with beaten egg yolk just before baking for a shiny crust.

Break Down:
1. Use dry yeast as directed on package.

Method 1:
Dissolve 5 mL (1 tsp.) sugar in 125 mL (½ cup) lukewarm water or milk. Sprinkle yeast over top and let stand 10 min then stir well. This mixture is called pre-dough.

Method 2:
Mix OETKER Dry Yeast directly with flour, sugar, salt in recipe.

2. Have all other ingredients such as eggs, butter, liquid, etc. at room temperature. Cold ingredients will retard the rising action of the dough.

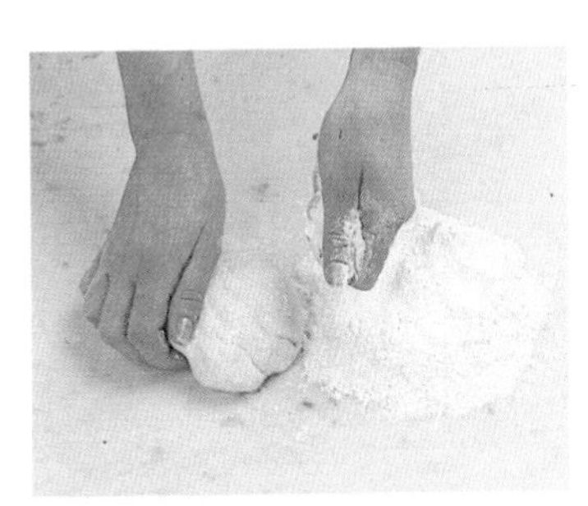

3. If a pre-dough is made, mix it with other ingredients and HALF the flour. Beat well until dough is smooth and slightly elastic. KNEAD the rest of the flour into the dough.

4. Knead dough until smooth and elastic. It will be shiny and blistered in appearance. You can knead the dough with both hands on a flat, floured surface such as a pastry board OR you can knead it right in the bowl using one hand to work the dough and the other hand to hold the bowl.

5. Place dough in a greased bowl, turning to grease top of dough. Cover with a cloth. Let dough rise in a warm place until doubled in size. The time for rising will depend on the temperature. You can also let dough rise overnight in the refrigerator without loss of flavour.

Recipe No. 1

Black Forest Cake

(Schwarzwaelder Kirschtorte)

Batter:

6	egg yolks	6
250 mL	sugar	1 cup
1 pkg	OETKER Vanilla Sugar	1 pkg.
30 mL	hot water	2 tbsp.
1 btl	OETKER Rum Essence	1 btl.
6	egg whites	6
125 mL	all-purpose flour	½ cup
50 mL	cocoa	¼ cup
45 mL	OETKER GUSTIN Corn Starch	3 tbsp.
5 mL	OETKER Baking Powder	1 tsp.
	Kirsch or brandy, optional	

Filling:

500 mL	whipping cream	2 cups
2 pkg	OETKER Whip-It	2 pkg.
45 mL	sifted icing sugar	3 tbsp.
2 pkg	OETKER Vanilla Sugar	2 pkg.
375 mL	Cherry pie filling	1½ cups
3 sq	semi-sweet chocolate, grated	3 sq.
	maraschino cherries	

Batter:
PREHEAT oven to 180°C (350°F). Grease and flour a 24 cm (9½″) spring form pan. Line with waxed paper.
COMBINE egg yolks, ⅔ of sugar, vanilla sugar, hot water and rum essence in mixer bowl. Beat at high speed of electric mixer until thick and creamy.
BEAT egg whites and remaining ⅓ of sugar to stiff peaks.
SIFT flour, cocoa, cornstarch and baking powder together.
FOLD into egg yolk mixture gently but thoroughly.
FOLD egg whites into egg yolk mixture gently.
TURN batter into prepared pan.
BAKE on lower oven rack at 180°C (350°F) for 45-50 min or until toothpick inserted in centre comes out clean.
REMOVE from pan immediately. Remove waxed paper and let cake cool completely.
SLICE cake in half horizontally with thread (Page 7) to make 2 layers. Drizzle bottom layer with brandy.
Filling:
BEAT cream in small mixing bowl to soft peaks. Gradually add Whip-It, icing sugar and vanilla sugar, beating to stiff peaks.
SPREAD cherry pie filling on bottom cake layer.
SPREAD ⅓ of cream mixture over pie filling. Place top cake layer over cream. Spread sides and top of cake with cream, reserving a small amount for decoration.
COVER sides with grated chocolate and sprinkle some on top.
DECORATE with whipped cream and cherries.

Recipe No. 2 (Picture Page 29)

Chocolate Cream Torte

(Schokoladencremetorte)

Batter:

325 mL	butter or margarine	1⅓ cups
250 mL	sugar	1 cup
1 pkg	OETKER Vanilla Sugar	1 pkg.
4	egg yolks	4
4	egg whites	4
425 mL	all-purpose flour	1¾ cups
15 mL	*OETKER Baking Powder	1 tbsp.
575 mL	ground walnuts	2⅓ cups

*1 pkg. OETKER Baking Powder is equivalent to 15 mL or 1 tbsp.

Batter:
PREHEAT oven to 160°C (325°F). Grease bottom of 26 cm (10½″) spring form pan.
CREAM butter. Gradually add sugar, vanilla sugar and egg yolks, beating until light and fluffy.
BEAT egg whites to stiff peaks.
Sift flour and baking powder together. Add to creamed mixture. Stir in ground nuts.
FOLD ½ of egg whites into creamed mixture, mixing well. Gently fold in remaining egg whites.
TURN batter into prepared pan.
BAKE on lower oven rack at 160°C (325°F) for 50-60 min or until toothpick inserted in centre comes out clean.
REMOVE from pan immediately and cool cake completely.
SLICE cake horizontally with thread to make 2 layers.
Continued on page 28.

Filling:

250 mL	milk	1 cup
1 pkg	OETKER Chocolate Frosting Mix	1 pkg.
325 mL	sweet (unsalted) butter	1⅓ cups
4 sq	semi-sweet chocolate, melted	4 sq.
1 btl	OETKER Rum Essence	1 btl.
375 mL	sifted icing sugar OR USE: Chocolate Cream I (Page 128)	1½ cups
75 mL	apricot jam	⅓ cup

Decoration:

1 sq	semi-sweet chocolate	1 sq.

Filling:
*Have milk and butter at room temperature.
COMBINE milk and frosting mix in small mixer bowl. Beat at high speed of electric mixer until stiff peaks form, about 4 min.
CREAM butter. Add chocolate frosting mixture, a spoonful at a time, beating until well blended. Beat in melted chocolate and rum essence, then icing sugar gradually, adding just enough to make a smooth creamy consistency.
OR Prepare Chocolate Cream I, adding essence.
SPREAD jam and half of filling on bottom cake layer. Cover with top cake layer. Spread frosting over sides and top of cake, reserving some for decoration.
DECORATE attractively with remaining filling.
GRATE 1 square chocolate coarsely. Sprinkle on centre of cake.

Recipe No. 3

Coffee Cream Torte

(Kaffeecreme-Torte)

Batter:

5	egg yolks	5
125 mL	sugar	½ cup
1 pkg	OETKER Vanilla Sugar	1 pkg.
5	egg whites	5
150 mL	all-purpose flour	⅔ cup
5 mL	OETKER Baking Powder	1 tsp.
150 mL	ground pecans	⅔ cup
50 mL	cooking oil	¼ cup

Filling:

250 mL	milk	1 cup
1 pkg	OETKER Coffee Frosting Mix	1 pkg.
30 mL	instant coffee powder	2 tbsp.
325 mL	sweet (unsalted) butter	1⅓ cups
300 mL	sifted icing sugar OR USE: Coffee Cream Filling I (Page 127)	1¼ cups
1 btl	OETKER Rum Essence	1 btl.
45 mL	mocha or coffee liqueur	3 tbsp.

Garnish:

finely chopped nuts
coffee beans or chocolate chips

Batter:
PREHEAT oven to 160°C (325°F). Grease bottom of 24 cm (9½") spring form pan.
COMBINE egg yolks, sugar and vanilla sugar together in mixer bowl.
BEAT at high speed of electric mixer until thick and creamy.
BEAT egg whites to form stiff but moist peaks.
SIFT flour and baking powder together over egg yolk mixture.
FOLD in gently but thoroughly.
FOLD nuts and egg whites gently into egg yolk mixture.
STIR oil in gently.
TURN batter into prepared pan.
BAKE on lower oven rack at 150°C (300°F) for 40-50 min or until toothpick inserted in centre comes out clean. Let cool in pan but loosen spring on pan.
SLICE cooled cake in half horizontally with thread (Page 7) to make 2 layers.

Filling:
*Have milk and butter at room temperature.
COMBINE milk, frosting mix and coffee in small mixer bowl. Beat on high speed of electric mixer until stiff peaks form, about 4 min.
CREAM butter with icing sugar, essence and liqueur until smooth. Gradually add frosting mixture, a spoonful at a time, beating until smooth and creamy.
OR Prepare Coffee Cream I, adding essence and liqueur.
SPREAD some filling on bottom cake layer. Place top cake layer over filling. Spread sides and top with remaining filling. Use a wet warm knife for easy spreading.
DECORATE sides of cake with chopped nuts and top with coffee beans or chocolate chips.

Recipe No. 4

Apple Cake

(Apfeltorte)

Filling:

8	small apples	8
125 mL	raisins	½ cup
30 mL	Rum	2 tbsp.
	OR	
2 btl	OETKER Rum Essence	2 btl.
15 mL	sugar	1 tbsp.
15 mL	grated chocolate	1 tbsp.
10 mL	butter or margarine	2 tsp.

Batter:

175 mL	butter or margarine	¾ cup
175 mL	sugar	¾ cup
1 pkg	OETKER Vanilla Sugar	1 pkg.
3	eggs	3
1 btl	OETKER Lemon Essence	1 btl.
300 mL	all-purpose flour	1¼ cups
5 mL	OETKER Baking Powder	1 tsp.
2 mL	cinnamon	½ tsp.

Decoration:

45 mL	ground almonds	3 tbsp.
30 mL	sugar	2 tbsp.
	apricot jam	
	sifted icing sugar	

Filling:
PEEL and core apples.
COMBINE raisins, rum, 15 mL (1 tbsp.) sugar and grated chocolate in small saucepan. Bring to a boil then set aside while preparing batter.

Batter:
PREHEAT oven to 180°C (350°F). Lightly grease bottom of 26 cm (10½") spring form pan.
CREAM butter, sugar and vanilla sugar together. Beat in eggs, one at a time and lemon essence, beating until light and fluffy.
SIFT flour, baking powder and cinnamon together. Gradually beat into creamed mixture.
TURN batter into prepared pan. Arrange apples on top of batter.
FILL apple centres with raisin mixture. Dot with 10 mL (2 tsp.) butter.
BAKE at 180°C (350°F) for 45 min. Sprinkle with a mixture of ground almonds and sugar. Bake 10-15 min longer, or until apples are tender.
REMOVE from oven. Brush jam over apple opening and sprinkle icing sugar over cake portion.

Recipe No. 5

Glazed Fruit Flan

(Obsttorte)

Batter:

75 mL	butter	⅓ cup
2	egg yolks	2
125 mL	sugar	½ cup
1 pkg	OETKER Vanilla Sugar	1 pkg.
45 mL	hot water	3 tbsp.
2	egg whites	2
225 mL	all-purpose flour	⅞ cup
5 mL	OETKER Baking Powder	1 tsp.

Filling:

1 pkg	OETKER Vanilla Pudding and Pie Filling	1 pkg.
625 mL	milk	2½ cups
50 mL	sugar	¼ cup
1 pkg	OETKER Vanilla Sugar	1 pkg.

Decoration:

500-750 g	any fresh fruit in season such as strawberries, grapes, blueberries OR canned fruit such as apricots, pears, peaches, pineapple, etc.	1-1½ lbs.

Glaze:

1 pkg	OETKER Clear or Red Glaze	1 pkg.
250 mL	water or fruit juice	1 cup
30 mL	sugar	2 tbsp.

Batter:
PREHEAT oven to 180°C (350°F). Grease and flour a 26 cm (10½") flan pan.
COMBINE butter, egg yolks, ⅔ of sugar, vanilla sugar and hot water. Beat at high speed of electric mixer until thick and creamy.
BEAT egg whites and remaining sugar to stiff peaks. Fold into egg yolk mixture.
SIFT flour and baking powder together over egg mixture. Fold in gently.
TURN batter into prepared pan. Make sure batter is down in grooves.
BAKE at 180°C (350°F) for 25-30 min or until toothpick inserted in centre comes out clean.
REMOVE from pan immediately. Place cold wet cloth on back of pan for easy removal of cake. Cool cake completely.

Filling:
USING all filling ingredients, prepare according to package directions.
Cool slightly then spread over cake.

Decoration:
ARRANGE fruit attractively over filling.

Glaze:
PREPARE glaze according to package directions. Spoon hot glaze over fruit. Chill to set.

Recipe No. 6

Torte Meran

(Meraner Torte)

***Recipe makes 1 layer. Double recipe if 2 layers are desired.**

Batter:

175 mL	butter or margarine	¾ cup
175 mL	sugar	¾ cup
1 pkg	OETKER Vanilla Sugar	1 pkg.
3	egg yolks	3
3	egg whites	3
175 mL	all-purpose flour	¾ cup
5 mL	OETKER Baking Powder	1 tsp.
375 mL	ground pecans or hazelnuts	1½ cups
3 sq	semi-sweet chocolate, grated	3 sq.

Spread:

50 mL	apricot jam	¼ cup

Glaze No. 1:

50 mL	butter or margarine	¼ cup
2 sq	semi-sweet chocolate	2 sq.

Glaze No. 2:

1 pkg	OETKER Chocofix	1 pkg.

Decoration:

125 mL	whipping cream	½ cup
1 pkg	OETKER Whip-It	1 pkg.
15 mL	sifted icing sugar	1 tbsp.
30 mL	Cherry Brandy	2 tbsp.

Batter:

PREHEAT oven to 160°C (325°F). Grease bottom of 24 cm (9½″) spring form pan.
CREAM butter, sugar, vanilla sugar and egg yolks together until light and fluffy.
BEAT egg whites to form stiff but moist peaks.
SIFT flour and baking powder together. Add to creamed mixture.
ADD nuts and chocolate, 30 mL (2 tbsp.) at a time, mixing well after each addition.
FOLD egg whites gently into creamed mixture.
TURN batter into prepared pan.
BAKE on middle oven rack for 50-60 min or until toothpick inserted in centre comes out clean.
COOL cake completely then remove from pan.
SPREAD top of cake with jam. If making a 2-layer cake spread jam between layers as well.

Glaze:

MELT butter and chocolate together over low heat until smoothly blended. Spread over jam and down sides of cake.
OR PUT pouch of Chocofix in boiling water. When chocolate inside pouch is soft, cut off corner and pour Chocofix over jam.

Decoration:

BEAT cream in small mixing bowl to soft peaks. Gradually add Whip-It, icing sugar and Cherry Brandy, beating to stiff peaks. Decorate top of cake with cream.

Recipe No. 7

Creamy Cheesecake Torte

(Quark Sahne Torte)

***Filling can also be used on a bought sponge cake flan base.**

Batter:

2	egg yolks	2
125 mL	sugar	½ cup
1 pkg	OETKER Vanilla Sugar	1 pkg.
45 mL	hot water	3 tbsp.
2	egg whites	2
225 mL	all-purpose flour	⅞ cup
5 mL	OETKER Baking Powder	1 tsp.

Filling:

1 box	OETKER Cottage Cheese Cake Filling Mix	1 box
500 mL	cold water	2 cups
500 g	ricotta cheese or dry cottage cheese	1 lb.
250 mL	whipping cream	1 cup
5 drops	OETKER Lemon Essence	5 drops
45 mL	sifted icing sugar	3 tbsp.

Decoration:

fresh or canned fruit

Batter:

PREHEAT oven to 180°C (350°F). Grease and flour a 26 cm (10½″) spring form or flan pan.
COMBINE egg yolks, ⅔ of sugar, vanilla sugar and hot water. Beat at high speed of electric mixer until thick and creamy.
BEAT egg whites and remaining sugar to stiff peaks. Fold into egg yolk mixture.
SIFT flour and baking powder together over egg mixture. Fold in gently.
TURN batter into prepared pan. Make sure batter is down in grooves.
BAKE at 180°C (350°F) for 25-30 min or until toothpick inserted in centre comes out clean.
REMOVE from pan immediately. Place cold wet cloth on back of pan for easy removal of cake. Cool cake completely.

Filling:

COMBINE all ingredients according to package directions, adding lemon essence and icing sugar as you are whipping the cream.
SPREAD cheese mixture on top of cake.
DECORATE attractively with fruit of your choice.

Recipe No. 8

Cherry Cake

(Kirschtorte)

Batter:

175 mL	butter or margarine	¾ cup
250 mL	sugar	1 cup
1 pkg	OETKER Vanilla Sugar	1 pkg.
4	eggs	4
½ btl	OETKER Lemon Essence	½ btl.
500 mL	all-purpose flour	2 cups
15 mL	*OETKER Baking Powder	1 tbsp.
30-45 mL	milk	2-3 tbsp.
500 g	fresh cherries, pitted OR	1 lb.
400 mL	can Bing cherries, pitted and drained	14 oz.

*1 pkg. OETKER Baking Powder is equivalent to 15 mL or 1 tbsp.

Topping:

50 mL	sifted icing sugar	¼ cup
1 pkg	OETKER Vanilla Sugar	1 pkg.
	cherries	

Batter:

PREHEAT oven to 160°C (325°F). Grease bottom of 24 cm (9½″) spring form pan.
CREAM butter, sugar, vanilla sugar, eggs and lemon essence together until light and fluffy.
SIFT flour and baking powder together. Beat into creamed mixture. Gradually beat in milk.
TURN batter into prepared pan. Place cherries on top.
BAKE at 160°C (325°F) for 55-60 min.
TURN cake out onto serving plate. Sprinkle with icing sugar and vanilla sugar. Decorate with cherries.

Recipe No. 9

Poppy Seed Torte

(Mohntorte)

Batter:

125 mL	butter or margarine	½ cup
150 mL	sugar	⅔ cup
6	egg yolks	6
1 pkg	OETKER Vanilla Sugar	1 pkg.
6	egg whites	6
250 mL	ground poppy seed (available at Deli)	1 cup
175 mL	ground almonds	¾ cup
5 mL	OETKER Baking Powder	1 tsp.
5 mL	cinnamon	1 tsp.

Filling & Decoration:

150 mL	red currant jam	⅔ cup
125 mL	whipping cream	½ cup
½ pkg	OETKER Whip-It	½ pkg.
30 mL	icing sugar	2 tbsp.
1 pkg	OETKER Vanilla Sugar	1 pkg.

Batter:

PREHEAT oven to 150°C (300°F). Lightly grease and flour a 24 cm (9½″) spring form pan.
CREAM butter, sugar, egg yolks and vanilla sugar together in a large mixer bowl. Beat at medium speed until light and fluffy.
BEAT egg whites to stiff peaks.
STIR poppy seeds, ground almonds, baking powder and cinnamon into creamed mixture.
FOLD ⅓ of egg whites into creamed mixture thoroughly then gently fold in remaining ⅔ of egg whites.
TURN batter into prepared pan.
BAKE at 150°C (300°F) for 60-65 min or until toothpick inserted in centre comes out clean.
REMOVE from pan and cool completely.

Filling:

SLICE cooled cake in half horizontally to make 2 layers. Spread bottom layer with 45 mL (3 tbsp.) jam. Cover with top layer. Spread remaining jam over top and sides of cake.
BEAT cream to soft peaks. Gradually beat in Whip-It, icing sugar, and vanilla sugar. Continue beating until very stiff.
DECORATE cake with whipped cream using a decorating bag for an attractive finish.

Recipe No. 10 (Picture Page 38 lower)

Hazelnut Cream Torte

(Haselnuss-Cremetorte)

Batter:

4	egg yolks	4
175 mL	sugar	¾ cup
1 pkg	OETKER Vanilla Sugar	1 pkg.
30 mL	hot water	2 tbsp.
1 btl	OETKER Lemon Essence	1 btl.
4	egg whites	4
300 mL	all-purpose flour	1¼ cups
10 mL	OETKER Baking Powder	2 tsp.

Filling & Frosting:

500 mL	whipping cream	2 cups
2 pkg	OETKER Whip-It	2 pkg.
75 mL	instant chocolate powder	⅓ cup
50 mL	icing sugar	¼ cup
2 pkg	OETKER Vanilla Sugar	2 pkg.
1 btl	OETKER Rum Essence	1 btl.
	cherry jam	
125 mL	ground hazelnuts	½ cup

Decoration:

whole hazelnuts

Batter:
PREHEAT oven to 180°C (350°F). Grease bottom of 24 cm (9½″) spring form pan.
COMBINE egg yolks, ⅔ of sugar, vanilla sugar, hot water and lemon essence in mixer bowl.
BEAT at high speed of electric mixer until thick and creamy.
BEAT egg whites and remaining ⅓ sugar to stiff peaks.
SIFT flour and baking powder together over egg yolk mixture. Fold in gently but thoroughly.
FOLD egg whites gently into egg yolk mixture. Do not stir.
TURN batter into prepared pan.
BAKE on lower oven rack at 180°C (350°F) for 35-45 min or until toothpick inserted in centre comes out clean.
REMOVE ring of pan while hot; let cake cool completely.
SLICE cooled cake in half horizontally with thread to make 2 layers.

Filling:
BEAT cream until almost stiff. Gradually add Whip-It, chocolate powder, icing sugar, vanilla sugar and rum essence, beating until stiff. Do not overbeat.
SPREAD half of jam on bottom cake layer. Spread some cream filling over jam. Place top cake layer over filling. Spread remaining jam on top layer. Reserve a little filling for decoration.
SPREAD sides and top of cake with cream mixture. Dip knife in warm water and smooth out cream on cake. Cover side of cake with ground hazelnuts.
DECORATE with rosettes from the reserved cream. Complete decoration with hazelnuts.

Recipe No. 11 (Picture Page 39 upper)

Glazed Nut Torte

(Glasierte Nusstorte)

Batter:

6	egg yolks	6
300 mL	sugar	1¼ cups
1 pkg	OETKER Vanilla Sugar	1 pkg.
500 mL	ground walnuts or hazelnuts	2 cups
6	egg whites	6
325 mL	all-purpose flour	1⅓ cup
10 mL	OETKER Baking Powder	2 tsp.

Batter:
PREHEAT oven to 160°C (325°F). Grease bottom of 26 cm (10½″) spring form pan or 24 cm (9½″) pan for a higher cake.
COMBINE egg yolks, sugar and vanilla sugar together in mixer bowl.
BEAT at high speed of electric mixer until thick and creamy. Stir in nuts.
BEAT egg whites to form stiff but moist peaks.
SIFT flour and baking powder together over egg yolk mixture. Fold in gently but thoroughly.
FOLD in egg whites.
TURN batter into prepared pan.
BAKE on lower oven rack at 160°C (325°F) for 50-60 min or until toothpick inserted in centre comes out clean.
REMOVE from pan immediately and let cake cool completely.
SLICE cake horizontally to make 2 layers.

Filling:

75 mL	apricot jam or marmalade	⅓ cup
1 btl	OETKER Rum Essence	1 btl.

Glaze:

500 mL	sifted icing sugar	2 cups
45-60 mL	lemon juice	3-4 tbsp.

Decoration:

walnut halves or whole hazelnuts

Filling:
COMBINE jam and rum essence. Spread on bottom cake layer. Cover with top cake layer.
COMBINE icing sugar and enough lemon juice to make a smooth paste.
SPREAD over top and sides of cake.
DECORATE with walnut halves.

Recipe No. 12 (Picture Page 38 upper)

Chocolate Coconut Meringue Torte

(Japonaise Torte)

Sponge Batter:

3	eggs	3
125 mL	sugar	½ cup
1 pkg	OETKER Vanilla Sugar	1 pkg.
30 mL	hot water	2 tbsp.
½ btl	OETKER Lemon Essence	½ btl.
125 mL	all-purpose flour	½ cup
2 mL	OETKER Baking Powder	½ tsp.

Coconut Meringue:

2	egg whites	2
1 mL	cream of tartar	¼ tsp.
125 mL	sugar	½ cup
1 pkg	OETKER Vanilla Sugar	1 pkg.
125 mL	coconut	½ cup

Filling:

2 sq	semi-sweet chocolate	2 sq.
250 mL	sweet (unsalted) butter	1 cup
250 mL	sifted icing sugar	1 cup
75 mL	sifted cocoa	⅓ cup
1 pkg	OETKER Vanilla Sugar	1 pkg.
2	egg yolks	2
45 mL	rum	3 tbsp.
1 btl	OETKER Rum Essence	1 btl.

Decoration:

75 mL	apricot jam	⅓ cup
125 mL	whipping cream	½ cup
½ pkg	OETKER Whip-It	½ pkg.
30 mL	sifted icing sugar	2 tbsp.
1 btl	OETKER Rum Essence	1 btl.

Sponge Batter:
PREHEAT oven to 180°C (350°F). Grease and flour two 24 cm (9½″) spring form pans.
COMBINE eggs, sugar, vanilla sugar, hot water and lemon essence in mixer bowl.
BEAT at high speed of electric mixer until thick and creamy, about 10 min.
SIFT flour and baking powder together over egg mixture. Fold in gently but thoroughly.
TURN batter into prepared pans.
BAKE at 180°C (350°F) for 20-25 min or until toothpick inserted in centre comes out clean.
REMOVE ring of pans while hot; let cake cool completely.

Meringue:
PREHEAT oven to 70°C (150°F). Line 24 cm (9½″) spring form pan with waxed paper.
BEAT egg whites and cream of tartar together to stiff but moist peaks. Gradually add sugar and vanilla sugar, beating to stiff peaks.
FOLD in coconut gently.
TURN meringue into prepared pan.
BAKE at 70°C (150°F) for 60-90 min or until firm and light golden. Cool slightly then remove paper from bottom.

Filling:
MELT chocolate to smooth consistency. Cool slightly.
CREAM butter. Gradually add icing sugar, cocoa, vanilla sugar, egg yolks and chocolate, beating until smooth.
BEAT in rum and essence.
SPREAD ⅓ of filling on one sponge cake layer on serving plate.
PLACE meringue layer over filling. Spread another ⅓ of filling over meringue and cover with other cake layer.

Decoration:
SPREAD jam over top of cake. Spread remaining filling around sides of cake.
BEAT whipping cream to soft peaks. Gradually add Whip-It, icing sugar and rum essence, beating to stiff peaks.
DECORATE top of cake with whipped cream mixture.

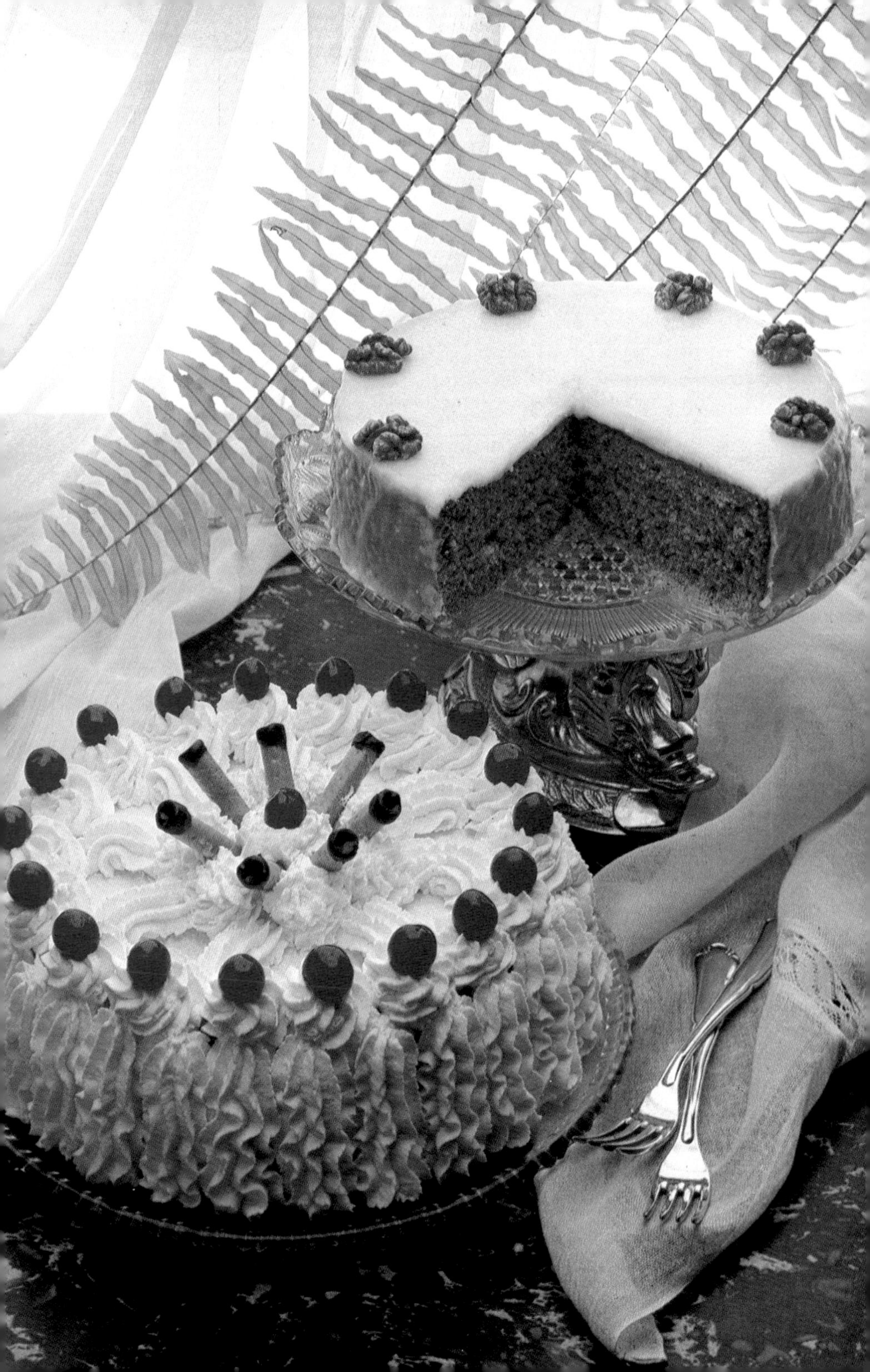

Recipe No. 13 (Picture Page 39 lower)

Malakoff Torte

Base:

1		orange	1
½		lemon	½
125	mL	water	½ cup
125	mL	sugar	½ cup
125	mL	rum	½ cup
70-80		lady fingers	70-80

Filling:

625	mL	milk	2½ cups
1	pkg	OETKER Vanilla Pudding and Pie Filling	1 pkg.
175	mL	sugar	¾ cup
250	mL	sweet (unsalted) butter	1 cup
30	mL	maraschino cherry juice	2 tbsp.
1	btl	OETKER Rum Essence	1 btl.
175	mL	ground Brazil nuts	¾ cup

Decoration:

375	mL	whipping cream	1½ cups
1½	pkg	OETKER Whip-It	1½ pkg.
50	mL	sifted icing sugar	¼ cup
2	pkg	OETKER Vanilla Sugar	2 pkg.
		rolled wafers, chocolate-dipped marachino cherries	

Base:
GREASE a 26 cm (10½″) spring form pan.
SQUEEZE juice from orange and half a lemon. Mix juices with water, sugar and rum. Bring to a boil then cool.
DIP lady fingers one by one, into cooled liquid. Line bottom of pan with a single layer of lady fingers. Sprinkle with some of the nuts.
Filling:
MIX 125 mL (½ cup) milk, pudding mix and sugar.
BRING remaining milk 500 mL (2 cups) to a boil. Take off heat. Stir in pudding mixture. Return to heat and bring just to a boil, stirring constantly.
COOL to room temperature, stirring occasionally.
CREAM butter. Gradually add cooled pudding, beating until smoothly blended. (Butter and pudding must be at same temperature to prevent curdling.) Stir in cherry juice and rum essence. Mix well.
SPREAD ⅓ of filling over lady fingers in pan. Sprinkle lightly with more of the nuts. Dip more lady fingers in orange liquid as before and place over filling. Repeat layering of filling, lady fingers and nuts, ending with lady fingers.
COVER pan with aluminum foil. Chill until set, 4 hr or overnight.
Decoration:
BEAT cream to soft peaks. Gradually beat in Whip-It, icing sugar and vanilla sugar, beating until stiff. Reserve some of the cream for decoration. Spread remaining on sides and top of cake. Decorate cake with reserved cream, using a decorating bag. Garnish with wafers and cherries.

Recipe No. 14

Valentine's Heart

Strawberry Heart Cake (Muttertagsherz)

Batter:

6		egg yolks	6
175	mL	sugar	¾ cup
2	pkg	OETKER Vanilla Sugar	2 pkg.
30	mL	hot water	2 tsp.
5	drops	OETKER Almond Essence, optional	5 drops
250	mL	all-purpose flour	1 cup
5	mL	OETKER Baking Powder	1 tsp.
6		egg whites	6

Batter:
PREHEAT oven to 160°C (325°F). Grease and flour a 26 cm (10½″) spring form pan.
COMBINE egg yolks, ⅔ of sugar, vanilla sugar, hot water and almond essence in mixer bowl. Beat at high speed of electric mixer until thick and creamy.
SIFT flour and baking powder together over egg yolks. Fold in gently but thoroughly.
BEAT egg whites and remaining ⅓ of sugar to stiff peaks. Fold into egg yolk mixture gently.
TURN batter into prepared pan.
BAKE at 160°C (325°F) for 45-55 min or until toothpick inserted in centre comes out clean.
REMOVE from pan immediately and let cool completely.
CUT cake into a heart shape. Slice in half horizontally to make 2 layers.
*Two layer cakes could be prepared from a white cake mix if desired. Bake in heart shaped pans if available, or use two 20 cm (8″) square pans and cut out the heart shape.
Continued on page 42.

ZUCKER
KAFFEE

Filling:

500 g	pkg. frozen strawberries or raspberries, thawed	15 oz.
500 mL	strawberry liquid from fruit	2 cups
75 mL	sugar	⅓ cup
1 pkg	OETKER Vanilla Pudding	1 pkg.
250 mL	sweet (unsalted) butter	1 cup

Glaze:

250 mL	sifted icing sugar	1 cup
30-45 mL	lemon juice	2-3 tbsp.

Decoration:

125 mL	whipping cream	½ cup
½ pkg	OETKER Whip-It	½ pkg.
30 mL	sifted icing sugar	2 tbsp.
1 pkg	OETKER Vanilla Sugar	1 pkg.

Filling:
STRAIN fruit to remove seeds. Add water to make 500 mL (2 cups) liquid.
COMBINE 50 mL (¼ cup) of the strawberry liquid, sugar and pudding mix until smooth.
BRING remaining strawberry liquid to a boil. Take off heat. Stir in pudding mixture. Return to heat and bring just to a boil, stirring constantly. Remove from heat. Cool to room temperature, stirring occasionally.
CREAM butter. Gradually add cooled strawberry mixture, beating until smoothly blended.
SPREAD ⅔ of filling on bottom cake layer. Place top cake layer over filling. Spread remaining filling around sides of cake.
Glaze:
MIX icing sugar with enough lemon juice to make a suitable glaze consistency. Spread evenly over top of cake.
Decoration:
BEAT cream to soft peaks. Gradually add Whip-It, icing sugar and vanilla sugar, beating to stiff peaks.
Decorate sides and around top edge of cake.

Recipe No. 15

Pistachio Cream Torte

(Pistazien-Cremetorte)

Batter:

4	egg yolks	4
250 mL	sugar	1 cup
1 pkg	OETKER Vanilla Sugar	1 pkg.
30 mL	hot water	2 tbsp.
5 drops	OETKER Bitter Almond Essence	5 drops
4	egg whites	4
300 mL	all-purpose flour	1¼ cups
1 pkg	OETKER Vanilla Pudding and Pie Filling	1 pkg.
15 mL	*OETKER Baking Powder	1 tbsp.
30-45 mL	milk	2-3 tbsp.

*1 pkg. OETKER Baking Powder is equivalent to 15 mL or 1 tbsp.

Filling:

1 pkg	OETKER Almond Pudding and Pie Filling	1 pkg.
125 mL	sugar	½ cup
625 mL	milk	2½ cups
250 mL	sweet (unsalted) butter	1 cup
45 mL	cherry liqueur	3 tbsp.
6 drops	OETKER Lemon Essence	6 drops

Glaze:

250 mL	red currant jam	1 cup

Decoration:

175 mL	ground pistachio nuts	¾ cup

Batter:
PREHEAT oven to 160°C (325°F). Grease bottom of 26 cm (10½") spring form pan.
COMBINE egg yolks, ⅔ of sugar, vanilla sugar, hot water and almond essence in mixer bowl.
BEAT at high speed of electric mixer until thick.
BEAT egg whites and remaining sugar until stiff.
SIFT flour, vanilla pudding powder and baking powder together over egg yolk mixture. Fold in gently but thoroughly.
FOLD egg whites gently into egg yolk mixture.
ADD milk gradually. Turn into prepared pan.
BAKE at 160°C (325°F) for 25 min then reduce heat to 150°C (300°F) for 10-15 min.
REMOVE from pan immediately and let cake cool completely.
SLICE cake horizontally to make 3 layers.
Filling:
PREPARE almond pudding, sugar and milk according to package directions. Cool to room temperature stirring occasionally.
CREAM butter. Gradually add pudding, beating until smoothly blended. (Butter and pudding must be at same temperature to prevent curdling.) Beat in cherry liqueur and lemon essence.
SPREAD bottom layer with ⅓ of jam and ⅓ of filling. Place second cake layer on top. Repeat jam and filling. Cover with top cake layer. Spread remaining jam on top and sides of cake. Cover sides with ground pistachio nuts.
DECORATE top with remaining filling.

Recipe No. 16

Dobostorte

Batter:

6	eggs	6
175 mL	sugar	¾ cup
1 pkg	OETKER Vanilla Sugar	1 pkg.
30 mL	hot water	2 tbsp.
250 mL	all-purpose flour	1 cup
5 mL	OETKER Baking Powder	1 tsp.

Filling:

325 mL	butter or margarine	1⅓ cups
325 mL	icing sugar	1⅓ cups
75 mL	cocoa	⅓ cup
1	egg yolk	1
1 btl	OETKER Rum Essence	1 btl.
7 sq	semi-sweet chocolate, melted	7 sq.

Decoration:

325 mL	sifted icing sugar	1⅓ cups
1 sq	semi-sweet chocolate, grated	1 sq.

Batter:
PREHEAT oven to 180°C (350°F). Lightly grease and flour five 24 cm (9½″) round cake pans.
COMBINE eggs, sugar, vanilla sugar and hot water in mixer bowl. Beat at high speed of electric mixer until thick and creamy.
SIFT flour and baking powder together over egg mixture. Fold in gently but thoroughly.
SPREAD in prepared pans, dividing evenly. If necessary, bake 2 or 3 layers at a time, keeping remaining batter in refrigerator.
BAKE at 180°C (350°F) for 10-15 min or until cake springs back when lightly touched.
LOOSEN edges and turn out of pan immediately. Repeat with remaining batter. Cool completely. Reserve one for glazing.
Filling:
CREAM butter. Sift icing sugar and cocoa into butter. Mix well. Beat in egg yolk and rum essence. Gradually add melted chocolate, beating until smooth.
Finishing:
RESERVE small amount of filling for decoration.
SPREAD filling evenly on 4 layers, laying one on top of the other to assemble cake. Spread on top and sides of cake. Dip knife in water to smooth top.
GLAZE reserved cake layer by melting 325 mL (1⅓ cups) icing sugar in metal pan until it is golden brown. Watch carefully.
SPREAD QUICKLY over reserved cake.
CUT QUICKLY with buttered knife into 10-12 wedges. Let cool then place on top of cake to look like a fan.
DECORATE with reserved filling using a decorating bag.
Grate chocolate square and press around sides of cake.

Recipe No. 17

Chocolate Almond Torte

(Othello-Torte)

Batter:

175 mL	butter or margarine	¾ cup
175 mL	sugar	¾ cup
1 pkg	OETKER Vanilla Sugar	1 pkg.
6	egg yolks	6
30 mL	hot water	2 tbsp.
6	egg whites	6
250 mL	all-purpose flour	1 cup
10 mL	OETKER Baking Powder	2 tsp.
325 mL	ground almonds	1⅓ cups
5 sq	semi-sweet chocolate, grated	5 sq.

Filling:

250 mL	whipping cream	1 cup
1 pkg	OETKER Whip-It	1 pkg.
50 mL	sifted icing sugar	¼ cup
1 pkg	OETKER Vanilla Sugar	1 pkg.
50 mL	apricot jam	¼ cup

Glaze:

1 pkg	OETKER Chocofix OR Chocolate Glaze II (Page 130)	1 pkg.

Batter:
PREHEAT oven to 160°C (350°F). Grease bottom of 23 cm (9″) spring form pan.
CREAM butter, sugar, vanilla sugar, egg yolks and hot water together until light and fluffy.
BEAT egg whites to stiff peaks.
SIFT flour and baking powder together. Beat into creamed mixture.
ADD ground almonds and grated chocolate. Stir well to blend.
FOLD in egg whites gently.
TURN batter into prepared pan.
BAKE at 160°C (325°F) for 40-45 min or until toothpick inserted in centre comes out clean.
COOL cake in pan then remove and cool completely.
CUT cake twice horizontally to make 3 even layers.

Filling:
BEAT cream to soft peaks. Gradually add Whip-It, icing sugar and vanilla sugar beating to stiff peaks.
SPREAD ⅓ of filling on bottom cake layer. Cover with middle cake layer and spread with ⅓ filling. Place top layer over cream filling.
SPREAD jam over top of cake.

Glaze:
PLACE package of Chocofix in boiling water to soften contents. Cut corner off package and pour over cake. OR Prepare Chocolate Glaze II and spread over cake.
PUT remaining ⅓ filling in decorating bag and decorate cake.

Recipe No. 18

Chocolate Cherry Bombe

(Mozartbombe)

Batter:

6	eggs	6
175 mL	sugar	¾ cup
1 pkg	OETKER Vanilla Sugar	1 pkg.
1 btl	OETKER Lemon Essence	1 btl.
250 mL	all-purpose flour	1 cup
5 mL	OETKER Baking Powder	1 tsp.

Batter:
PREHEAT oven to 160°C (325°F). Grease and flour a 23 cm (9″) metal bowl.
COMBINE eggs, sugar, vanilla sugar and lemon essence in top of a double boiler placed over simmering water.
BEAT well until thick and foamy.
REMOVE from heat and continue beating until mixture is cool.
SIFT flour and baking powder over egg mixture. Fold in gently.
TURN batter into prepared bowl.
BAKE at 160°C (325°F) for 40-50 min or until toothpick inserted in centre comes out clean.
COOL in pan 10 min then remove from pan and cool completely.
CUT cooled cake horizontally into 4 or 5 layers.

Continued on page 48.

Chocolate Cherry Bombe (cont.)

Filling:

375 mL	whipping cream	1½ cups
1½ pkg	OETKER Whip-It	1½ pkg.
75 mL	sifted icing sugar	⅓ cup
2 pkg	OETKER Vanilla Sugar	2 pkg.
398 mL	can of pitted red cherries, drained	14 oz.
50 mL	juice from cherries	¼ cup
50 mL	Cherry Brandy	¼ cup

Glaze:

125 mL	whipping cream	½ cup
5 sq	semi-sweet chocolate	5 sq.
45 mL	sifted icing sugar	3 tbsp.
1 btl	OETKER Rum Essence	1 btl.

Decoration:

30 mL	ground pistachio nuts	2 tbsp.
	maraschino cherries	

Filling:
BEAT cream to soft peaks. Gradually add Whip-It, icing sugar, and vanilla sugar, beating to stiff peaks. Finely chop cherries. Fold into cream.
COMBINE cherry juice and cherry brandy.
PUT cake layers together in order by sprinkling each with juice and spreading with filling, dividing evenly.
Glaze:
BRING cream and chocolate to a boil, stirring until smoothly blended. Cool, stirring occasionally.
BEAT in icing sugar and rum essence, beating until thick and creamy. Spread evenly over cake.
Decoration:
Decorate cake with pistachio nuts and cherries.

Recipe No. 19

Lord Pueckler Torte

(Fuerst Pueckler Torte)

Batter No. 1:

4	egg yolks	4
75 mL	sugar	⅓ cup
1 pkg	OETKER Vanilla Sugar	1 pkg.
4	egg whites	4
75 mL	all-purpose flour	⅓ cup
5 mL	OETKER Baking Powder	1 tsp.
250 mL	ground almonds	1 cup

Batter No. 2:

4	egg yolks	4
75 mL	sugar	⅓ cup
1 pkg	OETKER Vanilla Sugar	1 pkg.
4	egg whites	4
45 mL	all-purpose flour	3 tbsp.
5 mL	OETKER Baking Powder	1 tsp.
125 mL	ground almonds	½ cup
2 sq	semi-sweet chocolate, grated	2 sq.

Filling:

250 mL	sweet (unsalted) butter	1 cup
250 mL	sifted icing sugar	1 cup
1 pkg	OETKER Vanilla Sugar	1 pkg.
30 mL	juice from red cherries	2 tbsp.
45 mL	chopped cherries	3 tbsp.
	Cherry Brandy	

Glaze:

2 pkg	OETKER Chocofix OR Chocolate Glaze II (Page 130)	2 pkg.

Batter No. 1:
PREHEAT oven to 160°C (325°F). Grease and flour a 24 cm (9½″) spring form pan.
COMBINE egg yolks, ⅔ of sugar and vanilla sugar in small mixer bowl. Beat at high speed of electric mixer until thick and creamy.
BEAT egg whites and remaining ⅓ of sugar to stiff peaks.
MIX flour, baking powder and ground almonds together. Fold into egg yolk mixture gently.
FOLD egg whites into egg yolk mixture gently but thoroughly.
TURN into prepared pan.
BAKE on lower oven rack at 160°C (325°F) for 50-60 min or until toothpick inserted in centre comes out clean.
REMOVE from pan immediately and let cake cool completely.
Batter No. 2:
PREPARE batter same as No. 1, adding grated chocolate to dry ingredients.
Filling:
CREAM butter. Gradually beat in icing sugar and vanilla sugar alternately with cherry juice. Fold in cherries.
PLACE dark cake layer on serving plate. Spread with ⅔ of filling.
PLACE light cake layer over filling, pressing down lightly.
SPRINKLE cherry brandy over cake. Place package of Chocofix in boiling water to soften contents. Cut corner from pouch and pour on cake. OR Prepare Chocolate Glaze II and spread over top and sides of cake.
DECORATE with remaining ⅓ of filling using a decorating bag.

Recipe No. 20

Linzer Cherry Torte

(Linzer Kirschtorte)

Sponge Cake Batter:

2	egg whites	2
50 mL	sugar	¼ cup
1 pkg	OETKER Vanilla Sugar	1 pkg.
1	egg yolk	1
75 mL	all-purpose flour	⅓ cup

Pastry Base:

75 mL	all-purpose flour	⅓ cup
1 mL	OETKER Baking Powder	¼ tsp.
125 mL	ground almonds	½ cup
50 mL	sugar	¼ cup
1	egg yolk	1
50 mL	butter or margarine, cold	¼ cup

Filling:

50 mL	strawberry jam	¼ cup
30-45 mL	red wine	2-3 tbsp.
2	cans (400 mL/14 oz.) red sour cherries, drained	2

Glaze:

250 mL	juice from cherries	1 cup
125 mL	red wine	½ cup
125 mL	water	½ cup
125 mL	sugar	½ cup
2 pkg	OETKER Red Glaze	2 pkg.

Decoration:

125 mL	whipping cream	½ cup
1 pkg	OETKER Whip-It	1 pkg.
30 mL	sifted icing sugar	2 tbsp.
1 pkg	OETKER Vanilla Sugar	1 pkg.

Batter:

PREHEAT oven to 160°C (325°F). Grease a 24 cm (9½″) spring form pan. Line with waxed paper.
BEAT egg whites to stiff peaks. Stir in sugar, vanilla sugar and egg yolk.
SIFT flour over egg mixture. Fold in carefully.
TURN batter into prepared pan.
BAKE on middle oven rack at 160°C (325°F) for 20-25 min or until toothpick inserted in centre comes out clean.
REMOVE from pan and let cool completely. Pan can now be used for base.

Pastry Base:

PREHEAT oven to 180°C (350°F).
COMBINE flour, baking powder, ground almonds and sugar on pastry board. Stir well to blend. Make a well in centre.
PUT egg yolk in well. Work small amount of dry ingredients into yolk to form a paste.
CUT cold butter in small pieces over paste. Quickly work all ingredients into a smooth dough.
PRESS or roll dough on bottom of spring form pan (remove rim).
BAKE at 180°C (325°F) for 10-15 min or until light golden.

Filling:

SPREAD jam over baked pastry base. Place sponge cake over jam. Replace rim on pan.
SPRINKLE with wine. Arrange drained cherries on cake.

Glaze:

RESERVE 45 mL (3 tbsp.) cherry juice.
BRING remaining cherry juice, wine, water and sugar to a boil.
MIX 2 pkg. red glaze with 45 mL (3 tbsp.) cherry juice. Stir into boiling mixture. Bring to boil again, stirring constantly, then remove from heat and cool slightly.
SPOON glaze over cherries, letting it run down sides of cake. Chill in refrigerator.

Decoration:

REMOVE rim from pan.
BEAT cream to soft peaks. Gradually add Whip-It, icing sugar and vanilla sugar, beating to stiff peaks.
PUT into decorating bag with tube and decorate cake.

Recipe No. 21

Strawberry Cream Torte

(Erdbeer-Sahnetorte)

Batter:

6	egg yolks	6
175 mL	sugar	¾ cup
2 pkg	OETKER Vanilla Sugar	2 pkg.
30 mL	hot water	2 tbsp.
5-6 drops	OETKER Lemon Essence	5-6 drops
6	egg whites	6
250 mL	all-purpose flour	1 cup
5 mL	OETKER Baking Powder	1 tsp.

Filling:

500 mL	whipping cream	2 cups
2 pkg	OETKER Whip-It	2 pkg.
50 mL	sifted icing sugar	¼ cup
2 pkg	OETKER Vanilla Sugar	2 pkg.
175 mL	strawberry jam	¾ cup

Topping:

500 mL	fresh or frozen strawberries, halved	2 cups

Glaze:

1 pkg	OETKER Clear Glaze	1 pkg.
50 mL	sugar	¼ cup
250 mL	water or strawberry juice	1 cup
30-45 mL	brandy	2-3 tbsp.

Batter:
PREHEAT oven to 160°C (325°F). Grease and flour a 26 cm (10½″) spring form pan.
COMBINE egg yolks, ⅔ of sugar, vanilla sugar, hot water and lemon essence in large bowl.
BEAT at high speed of electric mixer until thick.
BEAT egg whites and remaining ⅓ of sugar to stiff peaks.
SIFT flour and baking powder together over egg yolk mixture. Fold in gently but thoroughly.
FOLD egg whites gently into egg yolk mixture.
TURN batter into prepared pan.
BAKE at 160°C (325°F) for 45-55 min or until toothpick inserted in centre comes out clean.
REMOVE from pan immediately and let cake cool completely.
SLICE cake horizontally to make 3 layers.

Filling:
BEAT cream in small bowl to soft peaks. Gradually add Whip-It, icing sugar and vanilla sugar, beating until stiff. DO NOT OVERBEAT. Reserve 175 mL (¾ cup) for decoration.
SPREAD ⅓ of jam on bottom cake layer. Cover with ⅓ of whipped cream. Repeat putting middle and top layer on cake.
DECORATE top attractively with strawberries.
COMBINE clear glaze, sugar, water and brandy. Prepare according to package directions for glaze. Spoon hot glaze over strawberries. Decorate with reserved cream.
CHILL in refrigerator until serving time.

Recipe No. 22

Chocolate Torte

(Mohrentorte)

Cake:

175 mL	butter	¾ cup
250 mL	sugar	1 cup
1 pkg	OETKER Vanilla Sugar	1 pkg.
1 btl	OETKER Rum Essence	1 btl.
4	egg yolks	4
3½ sq	semi-sweet chocolate, melted	3½ sq.
250 mL	all-purpose flour	1 cup
10 mL	OETKER Baking Powder	2 tsp.
4	egg whites	4

Filling:

125 mL	sweet (unsalted) butter)	½ cup
175 mL	icing sugar	¾ cup
1 pkg	OETKER Vanilla Sugar	1 pkg.
3	egg yolks	3
4 sq	semi-sweet chocolate, melted	4 sq.

Decoration:

chocolate shot, optional

Cake:
PREHEAT oven to 160°C (325°F). Grease and flour a 23 cm (9″) spring form pan.
CREAM butter, sugar, vanilla sugar and rum essence together in large mixer bowl. Gradually beat in egg yolks and melted chocolate.
SIFT flour and baking powder together over creamed mixture. Mix lightly.
BEAT egg whites to stiff but moist peaks. Fold into creamed mixture gently but thoroughly.
TURN batter into prepared pan.
BAKE on lower oven rack at 160°C (325°F) for 50-60 min or until toothpick inserted in centre comes out clean. Cool before removing from pan.

Filling & Assembly:
CREAM butter, icing sugar, vanilla sugar and egg yolks together, beating until light and fluffy. Gradually beat in melted chocolate.
CUT cake horizontally to make 2 layers. Spread ½ of filling on bottom layer. Cover with top cake layer. Frost entire cake with remaining filling. Garnish with chocolate shot.

Recipe No. 23

Chocolate Filled Jelly Roll

(Baumstamm)

Batter:

5	egg yolks	5
175 mL	sugar	¾ cup
1 pkg	OETKER Vanilla Sugar	1 pkg.
5	egg whites	5
175 mL	all-purpose flour	¾ cup
1 mL	OETKER Baking Powder	¼ tsp.

Chocolate Filling:

250 mL	milk	1 cup
1 pkg	OETKER Chocolate Frosting Mix	1 pkg.
325 mL	sweet (unsalted) butter	1⅓ cups
375 mL	sifted icing sugar	1½ cups
50 mL	sifted cocoa	¼ cup
	OR USE: Chocolate Cream I (Page 126)	
1 btl	OETKER Rum Essence	1 btl.

Decoration:

finely chopped nuts, optional (pistachio nuts, almonds or walnuts)

Batter:

PREHEAT oven to 180°C (350°F). Grease a 2 L (39 cm x 26 cm/15″ x 10″) jelly roll pan and line with waxed paper. Grease again.
COMBINE egg yolks, sugar and vanilla sugar in mixer bowl. Beat at high speed of electric mixer until thick and creamy.
BEAT egg whites to stiff peaks.
SIFT flour and baking powder together over egg yolk mixture. Fold in gently but thoroughly.
FOLD in egg whites gently.
SPREAD batter evenly in prepared pan.
BAKE on middle oven rack at 180°C (350°F) for 10-15 min or until toothpick inserted in centre comes out clean.
TURN out immediately onto tea towel sprinkled with sugar. Remove waxed paper off cake back. Rub with a cool, wet cloth if necessary. Roll up cake in towel immediately starting at narrow edge. Let cake cool completely in towel.

Chocolate Filling:

*Have milk and butter at room temperature.
COMBINE milk and frosting mix in small mixer bowl. Beat at high speed of electric mixer until stiff peaks form, about 4 min.
CREAM butter, icing sugar and cocoa until smooth. Gradually add frosting mixture, beating until smooth and creamy. OR Prepare Chocolate Cream I. Stir in rum essence.
UNROLL cake. Spread ⅔ of filling over cake and roll up again. Spread remaining filling over top and sides (not ends) of cake. Make lines with fork and sprinkle with chopped nuts.

Recipe No. 24

Cherry Cream Filled Jelly Roll

(Biskuitroulade mit Cherry Brandy-Creme)

Batter:

5	egg yolks	5
175 mL	sugar	¾ cup
1 pkg	OETKER Vanilla Sugar	1 pkg.
5	egg whites	5
175 mL	all-purpose flour	¾ cup
1 mL	OETKER Baking Powder	¼ tsp.

Filling:

625 mL	milk	2½ cups
1 pkg	OETKER Vanilla Pudding	1 pkg.
50 mL	sugar	¼ cup
250 mL	butter, softened	1 cup
175 mL	sugar	¾ cup
50 mL	Cherry Brandy	¼ cup
90 mL	red currant jam or jelly	6 tbsp.

Decoration:

1 pkg	OETKER Chocofix OR	1 pkg.
1 sq	semi-sweet chocolate	1 sq.
40 mL	butter or margarine	2 tsp.

Batter:

PREPARE cake as in recipe #23.

Filling:

COMBINE 50 mL (¼ cup) milk, pudding mix and 50 mL (¼ cup) sugar until smooth.
BRING remaining milk to a boil. Stir in pudding mixture. Bring to a boil again, stirring constantly, until thickened. Cool to room temperature, stirring frequently.
CREAM butter, 175 mL (¾ cup) sugar and cherry brandy. Gradually beat in pudding mixture. (Butter and pudding must be at same temperature to prevent curdling.)
UNROLL cake. Spread ⅔ of filling over cake and roll up again.
SPREAD remaining filling over top and sides (not ends) of cake. Mark lines with fork.

Decoration:

SOFTEN Chocofix in boiling water. Cut small corner off pouch. Swirl over cake.
OR MELT chocolate and butter until smooth. Drizzle over cake.

Recipe No. 25

Cherry Slices

(Kirschschnitten)

Batter:

175 mL	butter or margarine	¾ cup
175 mL	sugar	¾ cup
1 pkg	OETKER Vanilla Sugar	1 pkg.
6	egg yolks	6
5 sq	semi-sweet chocolate, melted	5 sq.
6	egg whites	6
250 mL	all-purpose flour	1 cup
5 mL	OETKER Baking Powder	1 tsp.

Filling:

250 mL	whipping cream	1 cup
8 sq	semi-sweet chocolate	8 sq.
75 mL	milk	⅓ cup
½ pkg	OETKER Chocolate Frosting Mix OR USE: Chocolate Cream I (Page 126)	½ pkg.
1 btl	OETKER Rum Essence	1 btl.

Topping:

50 mL	apricot jam	¼ cup
398 mL	can of pitted red cherries, drained	14 oz.

Glaze:

250 mL	juice from cherries (add water if necessary)	1 cup
50 mL	sugar	¼ cup
1 pkg	OETKER Red Glaze	1 pkg.

Batter:
PREHEAT oven to 180°C (350°F). Grease and line a 2 L (39 cm x 26 cm/15″ x 10″) jelly roll pan with waxed paper. Grease again.
CREAM butter, sugar, vanilla sugar and egg yolks together until light and fluffy. Mix in melted chocolate.
BEAT egg whites to stiff peaks.
SIFT flour and baking powder together. Gradually add to creamed mixture. Fold in egg whites gently.
TURN batter into prepared pan, spreading evenly.
BAKE on middle oven rack at 180°C (350°F) for 10-15 min or until toothpick inserted in centre comes out clean.
TURN out immediately onto waxed paper sprinkled with sugar. Remove waxed paper from cake bottom. Let cool completely. Cut lengthwise into 2 even strips.
Filling:
COMBINE whipping cream and chocolate in saucepan. Bring just to a boil, stirring constantly until smoothly blended. Let cool.
COMBINE milk, frosting mix, rum essence and cooled chocolate mixture in mixer bowl. Beat on low speed to blend then on high until mixture is smooth and fluffy. OR Prepare Chocolate Cream I, adding essence.
SPREAD ⅔ filling on one piece of cake. Lay other piece on top.
SPREAD jam on top of cake. Arrange drained cherries on top of cake, leaving 2.5 cm (1″) border all around.
Glaze:
MIX 50 mL (¼ cup) juice with sugar and glaze. Bring remaining juice to a boil. Stir in glaze mixture and return to a boil.
SPOON hot glaze over cherries.
Decoration:
SPREAD some of remaining chocolate filling around sides of cake.
PUT rest into decorating bag and decorate top of cake attractively.

Recipe No. 26

Chocolate Nut Slices

(Schoko-Nuss-Stangen)

Batter:

150 mL	butter or margarine	⅔ cup
150 mL	sugar	⅔ cup
3	egg yolks	3
3	egg whites	3
175 mL	all-purpose flour	¾ cup
5 mL	OETKER Baking Powder	1 tsp.
250 mL	chocolate chips	1 cup
175 mL	ground nuts (almonds, walnuts or pecans)	¾ cup

Decoration:

250 mL	coarsely chopped nuts	1 cup

Batter:
PREHEAT oven to 180°C (350°F). Grease a 2 L (39 cm x 26 cm/15″ x 10″) jelly roll pan.
CREAM butter, sugar and egg yolks together in large mixer bowl.
BEAT egg whites to stiff peaks.
SIFT flour and baking powder together over creamed mixture. Add chocolate chips and ground nuts. Stir well to blend.
FOLD in egg whites.
SPREAD batter evenly on prepared pan. Sprinkle with chopped nuts.
BAKE at 180°C (350°F) for 20-25 min or until golden.
CUT in 5 cm x 1 cm (2″ x ½″) slices while warm. Cool.

Recipe No. 27

Whipped Cream Slices

(Sahne-Cremeschnitten)

Pastry:

2 pkg	frozen puff pastry OR USE: Recipe for Puff Pastry (Page 17)	2 pkg.

Glaze:

325 mL	sifted icing sugar	1⅓ cups
15 mL	lemon juice	1 tbsp.
15-30 mL	hot water	1-2 tbsp.
50 mL	apricot jam	¼ cup

Pudding Filling:

625 mL	milk	2½ cups
1 pkg	OETKER Vanilla Pudding Mix	1 pkg.
50 mL	sugar	¼ cup
1 pkg	OETKER Vanilla Sugar	1 pkg.
125 mL	sweet (unsalted) butter	½ cup

Cream Filling:

250 mL	whipping cream	1 cup
1 pkg	OETKER Whip-It	1 pkg.
30 mL	icing sugar	2 tbsp.
1 pkg	OETKER Vanilla Sugar	1 pkg.

Pastry:
PREHEAT oven to 220°C (425°F). Grease a baking sheet.
THAW puff pastry according to package directions or prepare recipe.
ROLL out on floured board very thin. Cut pastry so you have 3 equal size pieces. Place on prepared baking sheet.
BAKE on lower oven rack at 220°C (425°F) for 7-9 min or until golden. Cool.

Glaze:
BEAT icing sugar, lemon juice and hot water together until smooth.
HEAT jam and spread over 1 pastry layer.
SPREAD glaze evenly over jam.

Pudding Filling:
COMBINE 50 mL (¼ cup) milk, pudding mix, sugar and vanilla sugar, mixing until smooth.
BRING remaining milk to a boil. Stir in pudding mixture. Bring to a boil again, stirring constantly. Remove from heat and cool to room temperature, stirring occasionally.
CREAM butter. Gradually add pudding, beating until smoothly blended. (Butter and pudding must be at same temperature to prevent curdling.)
SPREAD filling mixture evenly on 1 pastry layer. Cover with second pastry layer.

Cream Filling:
BEAT cream to soft peaks. Gradually add Whip-It, icing sugar and vanilla sugar, beating until stiff.
SPREAD evenly over second pastry layer. Place glazed pastry layer over cream filling.

Note: If desired, you can use only 1 type of filling. Double the receipe for the filling you prefer.

Recipe No. 28

Orange Slices

(Orangen-Schnitten)

Batter:

5	eggs	5
175 mL	sugar	¾ cup
1 pkg	OETKER Vanilla Sugar	pkg.
250 mL	all-purpose flour	1 cup
50 mL	cocoa	¼ cup
1 mL	OETKER Baking Powder	¼ tsp.

Filling:

250 mL	sweet (unsalted) butter	1 cup
250 mL	sifted icing sugar	1 cup
1 pkg	OETKER Vanilla Sugar	1 pkg.
125 mL	orange juice	½ cup

Decoration:

1 sq	semi-sweet chocolate, grated	1 sq.
	orange sections	

Batter:
PREHEAT oven to 180°C (350°F). Grease a 2 L (39 cm x 26 cm/15″ x 10″) jelly roll pan. Dust lightly with flour.
COMBINE eggs, sugar, and vanilla sugar in large mixing bowl or top of double boiler. Place over simmering water (bowl should not touch water).
BEAT until very thick and creamy. Remove from bowl and continue beating until mixture is cooled.
SIFT flour, cocoa and baking powder together over egg mixture. Fold in gently but thoroughly.
SPREAD batter evenly in prepared pan. (Mixture should be 1 cm (½″) thick).
BAKE at 180°C (350°F) for 10-12 min or until set. Cool.
CUT into 5 cm (2″) squares.
Filling:
CREAM butter. Gradually add icing sugar, vanilla sugar and orange juice. Put mixture in decorating bag with star tube. Cover 1 square with filling. Place another square on top. Cover with filling. Sprinkle with grated chocolate and decorate with an orange section.

Recipe No. 29

Paris Slices

(Pariser Schnitten)

Batter

4	egg yolks	4
250 mL	sugar	1 cup
1 pkg	OETKER Vanilla Sugar	1 pkg.
5 drops	OETKER Almond Essence	5 drops
1 mL	cinnamon	¼ tsp.
4	egg whites	4
50 mL	all-purpose flour	¼ cup
5 mL	OETKER Baking Powder	1 tsp.
500 mL	ground nuts (hazelnuts, pecans, almonds or walnuts)	2 cups

Filling:

250 mL	whipping cream	1 cup
8 sq	semi-sweet chocolate	8 sq.
1 btl	OETKER Rum Essence	1 btl.

Glaze:

1 pkg	OETKER Chocofix, softened	1 pkg.
45 mL	sweet (unsalted) butter, softened	3 tbsp.
	OR USE: Chocolate Glaze II (Page 130)	

Batter:
PREHEAT oven to 180°C (350°F). Grease a 2 L (39 cm x 26 cm/15″ x 10″) jelly roll pan and line with waxed paper. Grease again.
COMBINE egg yolks, ⅔ of sugar, vanilla sugar, almond essence and cinnamon in mixer bowl. Beat at high speed of electric mixer until thick.
BEAT egg whites and remaining ⅓ of sugar to stiff peaks.
SIFT flour and baking powder together over egg yolk mixture. Fold in nuts gently.
FOLD in egg whites gently.
SPREAD batter evenly in prepared pan. Batter should be 1 cm (½″) thick.
BAKE at 180°C (350°F) for 20-25 min or until toothpick inserted in centre comes out clean.
TURN out immediately onto waxed paper sprinkled with sugar.
REMOVE waxed paper from back of cake. Rub with a cold wet cloth if necessary. Cool. Cut into 8 cm x 3 cm (3″ x 1¼″) strips.
Filling:
Bring whipping cream and chocolate to a boil, stirring constantly. Cool, stirring occasionally.
ADD rum essence.
BEAT at high speed of electric mixer until thick. Put into decorating bag with star tube.
SPREAD half of filling on half of cake slices.
Glaze:
Mix softened Chocofix with butter until smooth. OR Prepare Chocolate Glaze II.
SPREAD over remaining cake slices. Let set.
Decoration:
PLACE glazed slices over filled slices.
DECORATE with remaining filling.

Recipe No. 30

Petit Fours

Chocolate, nut, coffee and lemon (Schokolade-, Nuss-, Kaffee- und Zitronen-Petit-Fours)

In this recipe you have a choice of several different kinds of fillings and glazes which are found on various pages in the book. The basic cake directions are given below. The rest is up to you as to which fillings and glazes you want to use.

Batter:

5	egg whites	5
5	egg yolks	5
175 mL	sugar	¾ cup
1 pkg	OETKER Vanilla Sugar	1 pkg.
225 mL	all-purpose flour	⅞ cup
1 mL	OETKER Baking Powder	¼ tsp.
	jam to spread on top of cakes before glazing	

Decoration

1. Chocolate Cream Filling, Page 126
   Chocolate or Cocoa Glaze, Page 130
2. Nut Cream Filling, Page 127
   Egg White Glaze, Page 130
3. Coffee Cream Filling, Page 127
   Coffee Glaze, Page 130
4. Vanilla Cream Filling, Page 126
   Lemon Glaze, Page 130

Pearl candies, maraschino cherries, nuts, coffee beans, etc. to decorate.

Batter:

PREHEAT oven to 180°C (350°F). Grease a 2 L (39 cm x 26 cm/15″ x 10″) jelly roll pan and line with waxed paper. Grease again.
BEAT egg whites to stiff peaks. Gradually add egg yolks, sugar and vanilla sugar, beating until thick and creamy.
SIFT flour and baking powder together over egg mixture. Fold in gently but thoroughly.
TURN batter into prepared pan, spreading evenly.
BAKE at 180°C (350°F) for 10-15 min or until cake springs back when lightly touched.
TURN out immediately onto waxed paper sprinkled with sugar. Remove waxed paper from back of cake. Cool. Cut into 2 equal pieces.
SPREAD 1 piece of cake with desired filling. Place other cake over filling.
CUT into desired shapes. Spread top of each cake with jam.
GLAZE with desired glaze to compliment filling.
DECORATE as desired.

Recipe No. 31

Sacher Squares

(Sacher-Wuerfel)

Batter:

175 mL	butter or margarine	¾ cup
175 mL	sugar	¾ cup
1 pkg	OETKER Vanilla Sugar	1 pkg.
6	egg yolks	6
5 sq	semi-sweet chocolate, melted	5 sq.
1 btl	OETKER Rum Essence	1 btl.
6	egg whites	6
250 mL	all-purpose flour	1 cup
5 mL	OETKER Baking Powder	1 tsp.

Filling:

125 mL	whipping cream	½ cup
5 sq	semi-sweet chocolate	5 sq.
50 mL	sifted icing sugar	¼ cup
1 btl	OETKER Rum Essence	1 btl.
50 mL	apricot jam	¼ cup

Glaze:

2 pkg	OETKER Chocofix OR Chocolate Glaze II (Page 130)	2 pkg.

Decoration:

whipped cream or
maraschino cherries

Batter:
PREHEAT oven to 160°C (325°F). Grease a 2 L (39 cm x 26 cm/15″ x 10″) jelly roll pan. Line with waxed paper. Grease again.
CREAM butter, ⅔ of sugar, vanilla sugar and egg yolks together until light and fluffy. Stir in melted chocolate and rum essence.
BEAT egg whites and remaining sugar to stiff peaks.
SIFT flour and baking powder together. Add to creamed mixture.
FOLD in egg whites, gently but thoroughly.
TURN batter into prepared pan.
BAKE on lower oven rack at 160°C (325°F) for 40-50 min or until toothpick inserted in centre comes out clean.
REMOVE from pan immediately onto waxed paper sprinkled with sugar. Remove waxed paper from cake bottom. Cut in half starting at long side. Cool completely.
Filling:
BRING cream and chocolate to a boil, stirring until smooth. Cool, stirring occasionally.
ADD icing sugar and rum essence, beating until thick and creamy.
SPREAD jam and filling on one of the cake pieces. Place remaining cake piece over filling. Cut into 7 cm (2½″) squares.
GLAZE with Chocofix, prepared according to package directions, or Chocolate Glaze II. Decorate with whipped cream or cherries.

Recipe No. 32

Cream Slices

(Johannisbeer – Schaumschnitten)

Batter:

6	egg whites	6
250 mL	sugar	1 cup
1 pkg	OETKER Vanilla Sugar	1 pkg.
5 drops	OETKER Lemon Essence	5 drops
150 mL	all-purpose flour	⅔ cup
1 mL	OETKER Baking Powder	¼ tsp.
250 mL	ground almonds	1 cup

Topping:

250 mL	whipping cream	1 cup
1 pkg	OETKER Whip-It	1 pkg.
30 mL	sifted icing sugar	2 tbsp.
50 mL	red currant jelly	¼ cup

Batter:
PREHEAT oven to 160°C (325°F). Grease and line a 2 L (39 cm x 26 cm/15″ x 10″) jelly roll pan with waxed paper. Grease again and dust lightly with flour.
BEAT egg whites to stiff peaks. Gradually add sugar, vanilla sugar and essence.
SIFT flour and baking powder over mixture; add almonds. Fold in gently.
SPREAD batter evenly in pan.
BAKE on middle oven rack at 160°C (325°F) for 20-25 min.
TURN out immediately onto waxed paper sprinkled with sugar. Remove waxed paper from cake bottom. Let cool completely.
Topping:
BEAT cream in small mixing bowl to soft peaks. Gradually add Whip-It and icing sugar, beating to stiff peaks.
STIR in jelly, reserving a little for decoration.
*CUT cake into 5 cm x 2.5 cm (2″ x 1″) slices.
Cover cake slices with rows of cream.
DECORATE with thin lines of reserved jelly.
*Cake can be decorated whole then cut later.

Recipe No. 33

Linz Slices

(Linzer Schnitten)

Pastry:

500 mL	all-purpose flour	2 cups
5 mL	OETKER Baking Powder	1 tsp.
300 mL	sugar	1¼ cups
1 pkg	OETKER Vanilla Sugar	1 pkg.
5 mL	cinnamon	1 tsp.
2 mL	cloves	½ tsp.
1	egg	1
1	egg yolk	1
1 btl	OETKER Lemon Essence	1 btl.
325 mL	cold butter or margarine	1⅓ cups
750 mL	ground nuts	3 cups
6	wheat flan wafers	6

Topping:

1	egg white	1
125 mL	raspberry or red currant jam	½ cup
75 mL	sliced or chopped almonds	⅓ cup
	sifted icing sugar	

Pastry:
PREHEAT oven to 150°C (300°F). Grease a 2 L (39 cm x 26 cm/15" x 10") jelly roll pan.
SIFT flour and baking powder together onto pastry board. Make a well in centre.
PLACE sugar, vanilla sugar, spices, egg and egg yolk and lemon essence in well in centre. Mix small amount of flour mixture into centre ingredients to make a thick paste.
CUT cold butter into small pieces over flour mixture.
ADD ground nuts. Working quickly from the centre, work all ingredients together to make a smooth dough. If dough is sticky, chill slightly for easy handling.
PRESS or roll ⅔ of dough onto prepared pan to cover it.
LAY wafers over dough and brush with slightly beaten egg white. Spread with jam.
ROLL remaining dough into pencil-like strips. Place over jam in criss-cross pattern.
BRUSH strips with slightly beaten egg white. Sprinkle with almonds.
BAKE on middle oven rack at 150°C (300°F) for 25-30 min or until golden. Cool in pan. Cut into pieces. Sprinkle with icing sugar if desired.

Recipe No. 34

Party Squares

(Party-Schnitten)

Batter:

4	egg yolks	4
175 mL	sugar	¾ cup
1 pkg	OETKER Vanilla Sugar	1 pkg.
1 btl	OETKER Rum Essence	1 btl.
4	egg whites	4
175 mL	all-purpose flour	¾ cup
5 mL	OETKER Baking Powder	1 tsp.
250 mL	chocolate chips	1 cup
250 mL	chopped nuts	1 cup
250 mL	raisins	1 cup

Decoration:

½ pkg	OETKER Chocofix, melted OR Chocolate Glaze II (Page 130)	½ pkg.
125 mL	sifted icing sugar	½ cup
	hot water	
	maraschino cherry halves, optional	

Batter:
PREHEAT oven to 180°C (350°F). Grease and flour a 2 L (39 cm x 26 cm/15" × 10") jelly roll pan.
COMBINE egg yolks, ⅔ of sugar, vanilla sugar and rum essence in mixer bowl. Beat at high speed of electric mixer until thick and creamy.
BEAT egg whites and remaining sugar to stiff peaks. Fold into egg yolk mixture.
SIFT flour and baking powder over egg mixture. Add chocolate chips, nuts and raisins. Fold all ingredients together until well blended.
TURN batter into prepared pan spreading evenly.
BAKE at 180°C (350°F) for 20-25 min or until set and golden. Cool.
Decoration:
DRIZZLE melted chocofix over product before cutting.
BLEND icing sugar with a bit of hot water to make a glaze consistency. Drizzle over products similar to chocofix. Let set. Garnish with cherry halves if desired.
CUT into squares to serve.

oetker
oetker

Recipe No. 35

Honey Cake

(Honigkuchen auf dem Blech)

Batter:

375 mL	liquid honey	1½ cups
75 mL	sugar	⅓ cup
1 pkg	OETKER Vanilla Sugar	1 pkg.
125 mL	butter or margarine	½ cup
30 mL	milk	2 tbsp.
2	eggs	2
5 drops	OETKER Bitter Almond Essence	5 drops
10 mL	pumpkin pie spice	2 tsp.
5 mL	instant coffee powder	1 tsp.
750 mL	all-purpose flour	3 cups
20 mL	OETKER Baking Powder	4 tsp.
250 mL	ground hazelnuts or walnuts	1 cup
75 mL	chopped candied lemon peel	⅓ cup

Glaze:

1 pkg	OETKER Chocofix OR Chocolate Glaze II (Page 130)	1 pkg.

Decoration:

blanched whole almonds
candied cherries

Batter:
PREHEAT oven to 180°C (350°F). Grease 3.5 L (33 cm x 23 cm/13″ x 9″) cake pan.
HEAT honey, sugar, vanilla sugar, butter and milk together over low heat just until smoothly blended. Do not boil. Cool.
ADD eggs, bitter almond essence, spice and coffee to honey mixture. Stir well to blend.
SIFT flour and baking powder together. Add to honey mixture 15 mL (1 tbsp.) at a time, mixing well after each addition.
STIR in nuts and peel.
TURN batter into prepared pan.
BAKE at 180°C (350°F) for 35-45 min or until toothpick inserted in centre comes out clean. Cool cake in pan.

Glaze:
PLACE Chocofix in boiling water to soften contents. Cut corner off pouch and pour over cake. OR Prepare Chocolate Glaze. Spread evenly over top and let run down sides.
DECORATE with almonds and cherries.

Recipe No. 36

Cream Cheese Slices

(Quarkschnitten)

Base:

175 mL	butter or margarine	¾ cup
150 mL	sugar	⅔ cup
1 pkg	OETKER Vanilla Sugar	1 pkg.
4	egg yolks	4
4	egg whites	4
75 ml	all-purpose flour	⅓ cup
5 mL	OETKER Baking Powder	1 tsp.
375 mL	ground hazelnuts or walnuts	1½ cups

TOPPING:

50 mL	raspberry jam	¼ cup
1 pkg	OETKER Cottage Cheesecake Filling Mix	1 pkg.
500 mL	water	2 cups
1-5 drops	OETKER Lemon Essence	1-5 drops
30 mL	icing sugar	2 tbsp.
500 g	ricotta cheese or dry cottage cheese	2 cups
250 mL	whipping cream	1 cup
125 mL	chopped almonds, toasted	½ cup

Base:
PREHEAT oven to 160°C (325°F). Lightly grease a 2 L (39 cm x 26 cm/15″ x 10″) jelly roll pan.
CREAM butter, sugar, vanilla sugar and egg yolks together thoroughly.
BEAT egg whites to stiff peaks.
COMBINE flour, baking powder and ground nuts. Stir into creamed mixture. Fold egg whites into batter gently but thoroughly.
SPREAD evenly in prepared pan.
BAKE at 160°C (325°F) for 25-30 min or until golden. Cool completely in pan.

Topping:
SPREAD base with jam.
BEAT cottage cheese mix, water, lemon essence and icing sugar together in large mixer bowl until well blended. Gradually add ricotta cheese, beating until smooth, about 3 min.
BEAT cream in small bowl to stiff peaks. Fold into cheese mixture.
SPREAD over jam on cake base. Sprinkle with toasted nuts.
CHILL 2-4 hours before serving. Cut into strips to serve.

Mehl
Feine Thea

Recipe No. 37

Apricot Streusel Cake

(Aprikosenstreuselkuchen)

Any fresh fruit in season can be used in place of apricots.

Batter:

250 mL	butter or margarine	1 cup
250 mL	sugar	1 cup
1 pkg	OETKER Vanilla Sugar	1 pkg.
3	eggs	3
1 btl	OETKER Lemon Essence	1 btl.
500 mL	all-purpose flour	2 cups
10 mL	OETKER Baking Powder	2 tsp.

Topping:

	apricots, peeled and halved OR	
2(400 mL)	cans apricot halves, well drained	2(14 oz.)

Streusel:

300 mL	all-purpose flour	1¼ cups
175 mL	sugar	¾ cup
1 pkg	OETKER Vanilla Sugar	1 pkg.
2 mL	cinnamon	½ tsp.
125 mL	butter or margarine	½ cup

Batter:

PREHEAT oven to 180°C (350°F). Grease a 3.5 L (33 cm x 23 cm/13″ x 9″) pan.

CREAM butter, sugar, vanilla sugar, eggs and lemon essence together until light and fluffy.

SIFT flour and baking powder together over creamed mixture. Stir well to blend.

TURN batter into prepared pan.

PLACE apricot halves with cut side down on batter.

COMBINE flour, sugar, vanilla sugar and cinnamon for streusel in bowl. Work in butter with pastry blender or 2 forks until mixture is crumbly.

SPRINKLE evenly over apricots.

BAKE at 180°C (350°F) for 40-50 min or until toothpick inserted in centre of cake comes out clean.

SERVE warm or cool.

Recipe No. 38

Glazed Coconut Pinwheels

(Kokosrollen)

Pastry Dough:

375 mL	all-purpose flour	1½ cups
15 mL	*OETKER Baking Powder	1 tbsp.
1	egg yolk	1
50 mL	evaporated milk	¼ cup
3 drops	OETKER Lemon Essence	3 drops
125 mL	sifted icing sugar	½ cup
1 pkg	OETKER Vanilla Sugar	1 pkg.
75 mL	butter or margarine, cold	⅓ cup

*1 pkg. OETKER Baking Powder is equivalent to 15 mL or 1 tbsp.

Filling:

250 mL	shredded coconut	1 cup
50 mL	sugar	¼ cup
15 mL	cocoa	1 tbsp.
1	egg white	1
30 mL	water	2 tbsp.
3 drops	OETKER Bitter Almond Essence	3 drops

Glaze:

175 mL	sifted icing sugar	¾ cup
15 mL	lemon juice	1 tbsp.
15 mL	hot water	1 tbsp.

Pastry Dough:

PREHEAT oven to 180°C (350°F). Grease a baking sheet.

BLEND flour and baking powder together on pastry board. Make a well in centre.

PLACE egg yolk, evaporated milk, lemon essence, icing sugar and vanilla sugar in well.

WORK a little flour into centre ingredients.

CUT cold butter into small pieces. Work all ingredients together quickly into a smooth dough.

ROLL out on floured board to a 25 cm x 30 cm (10″ x 12″) rectangle 1 cm (½″) thick.

Filling:

COMBINE all ingredients in bowl. Mix well. Spread over dough.

ROLL up dough from long side.

CUT into triangular pieces.

PLACE on prepared baking sheet.

BAKE on middle oven rack at 180°C (350°F) for 30-35 min or until set and golden. Cool.

Glaze:

COMBINE icing sugar, lemon juice and water, stirring until smooth.

SPREAD evenly over top and sides of cooled pastries.

Recipe No. 39

Old Vienna Bundt Cake

(Altwiener Guglhupf)

Pound Cake Batter:

300 mL	butter or margarine	1¼ cups
300 mL	sugar	1¼ cups
1 pkg	OETKER Vanilla Sugar	1 pkg.
4	eggs	4
1 btl	OETKER Lemon Essence	1 btl.
550 mL	all-purpose flour	2¼ cups
15 mL	*OETKER Baking Powder	1 tbsp.
125 mL	milk	½ cup
250 mL	raisins	1 cup
125 mL	ground almonds	½ cup

*1 pkg. OETKER Baking Powder is equivalent to 15 mL or 1 tbsp.

Decoration:

50 mL	sifted icing sugar	¼ cup
1 pkg	OETKER Vanilla Sugar	1 pkg.

Batter:

PREHEAT oven to 160°C (325°F). Grease and flour a 24 cm (9½″) bundt pan.

CREAM butter, sugar, vanilla sugar, eggs and lemon essence together until light and fluffy.

SIFT flour and baking powder together. Add to creamed mixture alternately with milk. Make 3 dry and 2 liquid additions, combining lightly after each.

STIR in raisins and nuts.

TURN batter into prepared pan.

BAKE on lower oven rack at 160°C (325°F) for 50-65 min or until toothpick inserted in centre comes out clean.

COOL cake in pan 10 min, then remove and let cool completely.

TO SERVE, sprinkle with mixture of icing sugar and vanilla sugar.

Recipe No. 40

Apple Strudel

(Wiener Apfelstrudel)

Dough:

500 mL	all-purpose flour	2 cups
30 mL	cooking oil	2 tbsp.
15 mL	vinegar	1 tbsp.
pinch	salt	pinch
150 mL	warm water	⅔ cup

Apple Filling:

1.5 kg	cooking apples	3 lbs.
250 mL	raisins	1 cup
125 mL	ground nuts	½ cup
175 mL	sugar	¾ cup
1 pkg	OETKER Vanilla Sugar	1 pkg.
pinch	cinnamon, ground cloves	pinch
50 mL	butter or margarine	¼ cup
175 mL	fine bread crumbs	¾ cup
175 mL	butter or margarine for brushing	¾ cup

Dough:

SIFT flour onto pastry board. Make a well in centre. Put oil, vinegar and salt into well.

COMBINE ingredients mixing from centre with a fork, adding enough water to make a stiff dough.

WORK dough until smooth, shiny and blistered in appearance.

(The trick in strudel is in working the dough. The more you work it the better it will stretch).

SHAPE dough into a small loaf. Brush lightly with oil. Cover with a thick cloth and let rest in a warm place for 1 hr.

PLACE a linen tablecloth over a large table. Sprinkle with flour.

ROLL dough thinly on cloth then start to pull the dough to stretch it. Stretch dough by putting it over the back of your hands and gently pulling outward in all directions.

STRETCH dough as thin as possible.

PREHEAT oven to 190°C (375°F).

Apple Filling:

Peel and slice apples thinly.

ADD raisins, nuts, sugar, vanilla sugar and spices. Stir well.

MELT 50 mL (¼ cup) butter. Add bread crumbs and cook until golden.

MELT 175 mL (¾ cup) butter.

BRUSH ¾ of melted butter over dough. Sprinkle buttered crumbs over ⅔ of dough. Cover crumbs with apple mixture.

ROLL up tightly starting at end with filling, using tablecloth to help you roll.

PLACE on greased baking sheet. Brush with butter.

BAKE on middle oven rack at 190°C (375°F) for 40-50 min or until crisp and golden.

BRUSH occasionally with remaining butter during baking. Cool.

SPRINKLE with mixture of icing sugar and vanilla sugar to serve.

Recipe No. 41

Turkish Teacake

(Tuerkischer Teekuchen)

Batter:

250 mL	butter or margarine	1 cup
250 mL	sugar	1 cup
1 pkg	OETKER Vanilla Sugar	1 pkg.
1 btl	OETKER Lemon Essence	1 btl.
4	eggs	4
750 mL	all-purpose flour	3 cups
15 mL	*OETKER Baking Powder	1 tbsp.
250 mL	milk	1 cup
125 mL	raisins	½ cup
125 mL	coarsely chopped almonds	½ cup
150 mL	coconut	⅔ cup
125 mL	chopped mixed candied fruit	½ cup

*1 pkg. OETKER Baking Powder is equivalent to 15 mL or 1 tbsp.

Decoration:

hot apricot jam
desiccated coconut

Batter:

PREHEAT oven to 180°C (350°F). Grease two 11 cm x 25 cm (4½" x 10") loaf pans.

CREAM butter, sugar, vanilla sugar, lemon essence and eggs together until light and fluffy.

SIFT flour and baking powder together over creamed mixture. Stir well.

STIR in milk, adding just enough to make a soft dough that will drop off spoon.

ADD raisins, almonds, coconut and fruit. Fold in gently.

TURN batter into 2 prepared pans.

BAKE at 180°C (350°F) for 50-60 min or until toothpick inserted in centre comes out clean. Remove from pan. Let cool.

SPREAD with hot apricot jam. Sprinkle with coconut.

Recipe No. 42

Nut Wreath

(Nusskranz)

Biscuit Dough:

175 mL	dry cottage cheese, sieved, or ricotta	¾ cup
45 mL	milk	3 tbsp.
1	egg yolk	1
90 mL	cooking oil	6 tbsp.
75 mL	sugar	⅓ cup
1 pkg	OETKER Vanilla Sugar	1 pkg.
5 drops	OETKER Lemon Essence	5 drops
500 mL	all-purpose flour	2 cups
15 mL	*OETKER Baking Powder	1 tbsp.
	pinch of salt	

*1 pkg. OETKER Baking Powder is equivalent to 15 mL or 1 tbsp.

Filling:

500 mL	ground nuts (hazelnuts, pecans or walnuts)	2 cups
175 mL	sifted icing sugar	¾ cup
5 drops	OETKER Bitter Almond Essence	5 drops
2	egg whites	2
½	egg yolk	½
30-45 mL	water	2-3 tbsp.

Glaze:

½	egg yolk	½
15 mL	milk	1 tbsp.

Dough:

PREHEAT oven to 180°C (350°F). Grease a baking sheet.

BEAT cheese, milk, egg yolk, oil, sugar, vanilla sugar and lemon essence together until smoothly blended.

SIFT flour, baking powder and salt together. Add half to cheese mixture. Mix well. Turn out onto floured board.

ADD remaining flour mixture, mixing with hands to a smooth dough.

ROLL out on floured board to 45 cm x 35 cm (18" x 14") rectangle.

Filling:

COMBINE filling ingredients, adding just enough water to make a paste-like consistency.

SPREAD filling over dough. Roll up lengthwise like jelly roll.

PLACE on greased baking sheet. Shape into a circle. Join end seams well.

BRUSH with mixture of ½ egg yolk and 15 mL (1 tbsp.) milk.

CUT triangles in top of ring with knife.

BAKE on middle oven rack at 180°C (350°F) for 30-40 min or until golden.

Recipe No. 43

Spice Cake

(Gewuerzkuchen)

Pound Cake Batter:

175 mL	butter or margarine	¾ cup
300 mL	sugar	1¼ cups
1 pkg	OETKER Vanilla Sugar	1 pkg.
4	eggs	4
2 btl	OETKER Rum Essence	2 btl.
625 mL	all-purpose flour	2½ cups
15 mL	*OETKER Baking Powder	1 tbsp.
5 mL	pumpkin pie spice	1 tsp.
175 mL	milk	¾ cup
250 mL	chopped nuts	1 cup
175 mL	raisins	¾ cup
125 mL	chocolate chips	½ cup

*1 pkg. OETKER Baking Powder is equivalent to 15 mL or 1 tbsp.

Glaze:

1 pkg	OETKER Chocofix OR Chocolate Glaze II (Page 130)	1 pkg.

Batter:

PREHEAT oven to 180°C (350°F). Grease and flour a 24 cm (9½″) bundt pan.

CREAM butter, sugar, vanilla sugar, eggs and rum essence together thoroughly.

SIFT flour, baking powder and spice together. Add to creamed mixture alternatively with milk.

STIR in nuts, raisins and chocolate chips.

TURN batter into prepared pan.

BAKE at 180°C (350°F) for 60-70 min or until toothpick inserted in centre comes out clean.

COOL cake in pan 20 min then remove to rack and cool completely.

Glaze:

SOFTEN Chocofix as directed OR Prepare Chocolate Glaze II. Spread evenly over cake.

Recipe No. 44

Pecan Nut Ring

(Haselnuss-Ring)

Pound Cake Batter:

125 mL	butter or margarine	½ cup
175 L	sugar	¾ cup
1 pkg	OETKER Vanilla Sugar	1 pkg.
3	eggs	3
250 mL	all-purpose flour	1 cup
15 mL	*OETKER Baking Powder	1 tbsp.
1 mL	cinnamon	¼ tsp.
50 mL	milk	¼ cup
375 mL	ground pecans	1½ cups
125 mL	chocolate chips	½ cup

*1 pkg. OETKER Baking Powder is equivalent to 15 mL or 1 tbsp.

Glaze:

50 mL	apricot jam	¼ cup
550 mL	sifted icing sugar	2¼ cups
45 mL	hot water	3 tbsp.
1 btl	OETKER Rum Essence	1 btl.

Batter:

PREHEAT Oven to 160°C (325°F). Grease a 24 cm (9½″) spring form pan with centre insert to make a ring.

CREAM butter, sugar, vanilla sugar and eggs together until light and fluffy.

SIFT flour, baking powder and cinnamon together over creamed mixture. Stir well.

STIR in milk, nuts and chocolate chips.

TURN batter into prepared pan.

BAKE at 160°C (325°F) for 50-65 min or until toothpick inserted in centre comes out clean.

REMOVE cake from pan while warm. Let cool.

Glaze:

BRUSH cake with jam.

COMBINE icing sugar, hot water and rum essence to make a thick glaze consistency. Spread over cake to glaze.

Recipe No. 45

Chocolate Almond Log

(Rehruecken)

Batter:

45 mL	fine dry bread crumbs	3 tbsp.
175 mL	butter	¾ cup
175 mL	sugar	¾ cup
1 pkg	OETKER Vanilla Sugar	1 pkg.
4	eggs	4
3 sq	semi-sweet chocolate, melted	3 sq.
125 mL	ground almonds	½ cup
150 mL	all-purpose flour	⅔ cup
10 mL	OETKER Baking Powder	2 tsp.
1 pkg	OETKER Chocolate Pudding and Pie Filling	1 pkg.
30-45 mL	milk	2-3 tbsp.

Glaze:

1 pkg	OETKER Chocofix OR Chocolate Glaze II (Page 130)	1 pkg.

Decoration:

slivered blanched almonds

Batter:

PREHEAT oven to 160°C (325°F). Grease an elegant loaf pan. Sprinkle with bread crumbs. Shake out excess.

CREAM butter, sugar, vanilla sugar and eggs together until light and fluffy.

STIR in chocolate and almonds.

SIFT flour, baking powder and pudding and pie filling mix together over creamed mixture. Mix well.

ADD milk so batter drops off spoon.

TURN batter into prepared pan.

BAKE on lower oven rack at 160°C (325°F) for 50-60 min or until toothpick inserted in centre comes out clean.

REMOVE from pan and cool cake completely.

Glaze:

SOFTEN Chocofix as directed on package or prepare Chocolate Glaze II. SPREAD over cake. Decorate with almonds.

Recipe No. 46

Advent Nut Wreath

(Adventkuchen)

Batter:

200 mL	liquid honey	¾ cup
175 mL	sugar	⅔ cup
1 pkg	OETKER Vanilla Sugar	1 pkg.
3	eggs	3
250 mL	all-purpose flour	1 cup
5 mL	OETKER Baking Powder	1 tsp.
5 mL	ground cinnamon	1 tsp.
2 mL	ground cloves	½ tsp.
550 mL	ground walnuts, hazelnuts or pecans	2¼ cups

Glaze:

45 mL	red jam, heated	3 tbsp.
125 mL	sifted icing sugar	½ cup
15 mL	hot water	1 tbsp.

Decoration:

silver or gold sugar pearls

Batter:
PREHEAT oven to 180°C (350°F). Grease and flour a fancy cake pan or bundt pan.
WARM honey and sugar together. Do not boil. Let cool.
ADD vanilla sugar and eggs. Stir well to blend.
SIFT flour, baking powder, cinnamon and cloves together.
ADD to honey mixture. Gradually add nuts. Mix well. Let batter stand ½ hr then turn into prepared pan.
BAKE on lower oven rack at 180°C (350°F) for 70-80 min (for bundt pan 55-75 min) or until toothpick inserted in centre comes out clean.
REMOVE cake from pan and brush with hot jam.
COMBINE icing sugar and hot water to make a thick paste-like consistency. Pour over cake. Decorate with sugar pearls.

Recipe No. 47

Chocolate Ring Cake

(Pralinen-Ring)

Batter:

45 mL	fine dry bread crumbs	3 tbsp.
175 mL	butter or margarine	¾ cup
175 mL	sugar	¾ cup
1 pkg	OETKER Vanilla Sugar	1 pkg.
3	egg yolks	3
3 sq	semi-sweet chocolate, melted	3 sq.
425 mL	all-purpose flour	1¾ cups
15 mL	*OETKER Baking Powder	1 tbsp.
125 mL	milk	½ cup
3	egg whites	3

*1 pkg. OETKER Baking Powder is equivalent to 15 mL or 1 tbsp.

Filling:

375 mL	milk	1½ cups
1 pkg	OETKER Chocolate Frosting Mix	1 pkg.
325 mL	sweet (unsalted) butter	1⅓ cups
325 mL	sifted icing sugar	1⅓ cups
50 mL	sifted cocoa	¼ cup
	OR USE: Chocolate Cream I (Page 126)	
1 btl	OETKER Rum Essence	1 btl.

Decoration:

1 sq	semi-sweet chocolate	1 sq.
7 mL	butter	1½ tsp.
	chocolate covered candies	

Batter:
PREHEAT oven to 180°C (350°F). Grease 24 cm (9½″) spring form pan with insert. Sprinkle with bread crumbs. Shake out excess.
CREAM butter, sugar, vanilla sugar and egg yolks together until light and fluffy.
STIR in melted chocolate.
SIFT flour and baking powder together. Add alternately with milk to creamed mixture.
BEAT egg whites to stiff peaks. Fold into batter.
TURN batter into prepared pan.
BAKE on lower oven rack at 180°C (350°F) for 50-60 min or until toothpick inserted in centre comes out clean. Remove from pan and cool cake completely.
SLICE cake in half horizontally to make 2 layers.

Filling:
*HAVE milk and butter at room temperature.
COMBINE milk and frosting mix in small mixer bowl. Beat at high speed of electric mixer until stiff peaks form, about 4 min.
LET SIT at room temperature for 15 min.
CREAM butter. Add chocolate frosting mixture, a spoonful at a time, beating until well blended. Gradually add icing sugar, cocoa and rum essence, beating until smooth and creamy.
OR Prepare Chocolate Cream I.
SPREAD ½ of filling on bottom cake layer. Place top cake layer over filling. Cover cake completely with filling, reserving some for decoration.

Decoration:
MELT chocolate and butter together. Decorate in thin lines around cake.
PIPE rosettes of reserved filling around top of cake. Place chocolate candy in each rosette.

Recipe No. 48

Ladies Kisses

(Haselnusskuesse)

Ingredients:

3	egg whites	3
1 mL	cream of tartar	¼ tsp.
125 mL	sugar	½ cup
1 pkg	OETKER Vanilla Sugar	1 pkg.
1 mL	cinnamon	¼ tsp.
250 mL	ground nuts	1 cup
50 mL	finely chopped candied lemon peel	¼ cup

Method:

PREHEAT oven to 70°C (150°F). Line baking sheet with waxed paper.
COMBINE egg whites, cream of tartar, sugar and vanilla sugar in top of double boiler. Place over simmering water. (Pot bottom should not touch the water.)
BEAT with electric mixer until very thick.
FOLD remaining ingredients into egg whites.
DROP by small spoonfuls onto prepared baking sheet.
BAKE at 70°C (150°F) for 70-80 min or until light golden.
MAKES about 4 dozen.

Recipe No. 49

Wondernuts

(Wundernuesschen)

Ingredients:

2	egg whites	2
125 mL	sugar	½ cup
1 pkg	OETKER Vanilla Sugar	1 pkg.
4 drops	OETKER Bitter Almond Essence	4 drops
425 mL	ground hazelnuts or walnuts	1¾ cups

Decoration:

candied cherries, nuts or chocolate chips

Method:

PREHEAT oven to 140°C (290°F). Line baking sheet with waxed paper.
BEAT egg whites to soft peaks. Gradually add sugar, vanilla sugar and bitter almond essence, beating until very stiff.
FOLD in ground nuts.
SHAPE mixture into small balls. Place on prepared baking sheet.
PRESS cherry, nut or desired centre in cookie.
BAKE on middle oven rack at 140°C (290°F) for 20-25 min or until set and light golden. Cool slightly then remove from paper. Cool completely. Store in airtight container.
MAKES about 3 dozen.

Recipe No. 50

Nut Cookies

(Nusskrapferln)

Dough:

250 mL	all-purpose flour	1 cup
175 mL	sugar	¾ cup
1 pkg	OETKER Vanilla Sugar	1 pkg.
375 mL	ground walnuts, pecans or hazelnuts	1½ cups
2	egg yolks	2
5 drops	OETKER Lemon Essence	5 drops
175 mL	butter or margarine, cold	¾ cup
2	egg whites, lightly beaten	2

Decoration:

hazelnuts, halved

Method:

PREHEAT oven to 140°C (290°F). Grease a baking sheet.
COMBINE flour, sugar, vanilla sugar and ground nuts on pastry board. Make a well in centre.
PUT egg yolks and lemon essence in well.
GRADUALLY work dry ingredients into egg yolk mixture.
CUT cold butter into small pieces.
QUICKLY work into flour mixture to form a smooth dough.
SHAPE dough into small balls. Dip into egg white and place on prepared baking sheet. Press hazelnut into centre of each cookie.
BAKE on middle oven rack at 140°C (290°F) for 20-30 min or until light golden. Cool slightly then remove from sheet. Cool completely. Store in airtight container.
MAKES about 4 dozen.

Recipe No. 51

Brandy Glazed Nut Cookies

(Nusstoertchen)

Cookie Dough:

500 mL	all-purpose flour	2 cups
15 mL	*OETKER Baking Powder	1 tbsp.
125 mL	sugar	½ cup
1 pkg	OETKER Vanilla Sugar	1 pkg.
300 mL	ground pecans, walnuts or hazelnuts	1¼ cups
1	egg	1
1	egg yolk	1
175 mL	butter or margarine, cold	¾ cup

*1 pkg. OETKER Baking Powder is equivalent to 15 mL or 1 tbsp.

Filling:

250 mL	apricot jam	1 cup

Glaze:

325 mL	sifted icing sugar	1⅓ cups
30-45 mL	brandy	2-3 tbsp.
15 mL	hot water	1 tbsp.

Decoration:

30	candied cherries	30

Dough:

PREHEAT oven to 180°C (350°F). Grease 2 baking sheets.

BLEND flour, baking powder, sugar, vanilla sugar and nuts together on pastry board. Make a well in centre.

PUT egg and egg yolk in well. Work some of dry ingredients into egg.

CUT cold butter into small pieces. Work quickly into flour mixture to make a smooth dough. Do not overwork.

ROLL out dough on floured surface to .5 cm (¼″) thickness. Cut in 5 cm (2″) rounds. Place on prepared baking sheets.

BAKE on middle oven rack at 180°C (350°F) for 20-25 min or until light golden. Cool.

SPREAD jam on half of cookies. Place remaining cookies over jam.

Glaze:

COMBINE all glaze ingredients until smooth. Spread over cookies.

DECORATE with candied cherry in centre.

MAKES about 2½ dozen.

Recipe No. 52

Chocolate Almond Rounds

(Zuericher Moepsli)

Cookie Dough:

500 mL	all-purpose flour	2 cups
5 mL	OETKER Baking Powder	1 tsp.
150 mL	sugar	⅔ cup
1 pkg	OETKER Vanilla Sugar	1 pkg.
375 mL	ground almonds	1½ cups
1	egg	1
175 mL	butter or margarine, cold	¾ cup

Filling:

250 mL	apricot jam or marmalade	1 cup

Decoration:

125 mL	chocolate sprinkles	½ cup

Dough:

PREHEAT oven to 180°C (350°F). Grease 2 baking sheets.

BLEND flour, baking powder, sugar, vanilla sugar and almonds together on pastry board. Make well in centre.

PUT egg into well. Work a little of dry ingredients into egg.

CUT cold butter into small pieces. Work quickly into flour mixture to make a smooth dough. Do not overwork.

ROLL out dough on floured surface to .5 cm (¼″) thickness.

CUT into 5 cm (2″) rounds. Place on prepared baking sheets.

BAKE on middle oven rack at 180°C (350°F) for 10-12 min or until light golden. Cool.

SPREAD jam on half of cookies. Place remaining cookies over jam.

ROLL cookies in chocolate sprinkles to decorate.

MAKES about 2½ dozen.

Recipe No. 53

Fruit & Nut Strips

(Fruchtschnitten)

Ingredients:

3	eggs	3
150 mL	sugar	⅔ cup
1 pkg	OETKER Vanilla Sugar	1 pkg.
150 mL	all-purpose flour	⅔ cup
1 mL	OETKER Baking Powder	¼ tsp.
250 mL	coarsely chopped nuts	1 cup
175 mL	raisins	¾ cup
125 mL	chopped candied orange peel	½ cup
50 mL	chopped candied lemon peel	¼ cup
50 mL	chopped candied cherries	¼ cup

Method:

PREHEAT oven to 160°C (325°F). Grease a 2 L (39 cm x 26 cm/15″ x 10″) jelly roll pan.
BEAT eggs, sugar and vanilla sugar on high speed of electric mixer until thick and creamy.
SIFT flour and baking powder together over egg mixture. Mix well.
ADD nuts and fruit. Stir well to blend.
SPREAD batter evenly in prepared pan.
BAKE at 160°C (325°F) for 20-25 min or until set and golden.
CUT into 5 cm x 1 cm (2″ x ½″) strips while warm. Cool then remove from pan.

Recipe No. 54

Walnut Rounds

(Gefuellte Nusscheiben)

Cookie Dough:

250 mL	all-purpose flour	1 cup
5 mL	OETKER Baking Powder	1 tsp.
50 mL	sugar	¼ cup
1 pkg	OETKER Vanilla Sugar	1 pkg.
1	egg	1
15-30 mL	milk	1-2 tbsp.
175 mL	butter or margarine, cold	¾ cup
175 mL	ground walnuts	¾ cup

Filling:

125 mL	red currant or raspberry jam	½ cup

Decoration:

60-70 mL	sifted icing sugar	4-5 tbsp.
1 pkg	OETKER Vanilla Sugar	1 pkg.

Dough:

PREHEAT oven to 180°C (350°F). Grease a baking sheet.
COMBINE flour, baking powder, sugar and vanilla sugar together on pastry board. Make a well in centre.
PUT egg and milk in well. Work a little of dry ingredients into egg mixture.
CUT cold butter in small pieces over flour mixture. Add nuts.
WORK all ingredients together quickly to make a smooth dough. Chill slightly for easy rolling (about ½ hr).
ROLL out dough on floured surface to .5 cm (¼″) thickness.
CUT into 5 cm (2″) rounds. Cut 3 small holes with floured thimble in half the cookie rounds. Place on prepared baking sheet.
BAKE on middle oven rack at 180°C (350°F) for 10-15 min or until light golden. Cool.
SPREAD jam on solid rounds. Place rounds with holes over jam.
SPRINKLE with mixture of icing sugar and vanilla sugar.
MAKES about 2 dozen.

Recipe No. 55

Chocolate Crescents

(Schokoladenkipferl)

Cookie Dough:

250 mL	all-purpose flour	1 cup
75 mL	sugar	⅓ cup
2 pkg	OETKER Vanilla Sugar	2 pkg.
1	egg yolk	1
125 mL	butter or margarine, cold	½ cup
250 mL	ground walnuts	1 cup
1½ sq	semi-sweet chocolate, grated	1½ sq.

Glaze:

425 mL	sifted icing sugar	1¾ cups
75 mL	cocoa	⅓ cup
45 mL	butter or margarine	3 tbsp.
45 mL	hot water	3 tbsp.

Dough:

PREHEAT oven to 150°C (300°F). Grease a baking sheet.

COMBINE flour, sugar and vanilla sugar on pastry board. Make well in centre.

PUT egg yolk in well. Work a little of dry ingredients into egg yolk.

CUT butter into small pieces. Work quickly into flour mixture to make a smooth dough. Do not overwork.

ROLL dough, a little at a time, into long pencil-like strips. Cut into smaller 5 cm (2″) strips.

PLACE on prepared baking sheet. Shape into crescents.

BAKE on middle oven rack at 150°C (300°F) for 12-15 min or until light golden. Cool.

Glaze:

COMBINE all glaze ingredients in small saucepan. Heat on low, stirring constantly just until melted and smooth.

DIP cooled cookies in warm glaze. Place on rack to dry.

MAKES about 8 dozen.

Recipe No. 56

Almond Crescents

(Vanillekipferl)

Cookie Dough:

425 mL	all-purpose flour	1¾ cups
250 mL	ground almonds	1 cup
50 mL	sugar	¼ cup
1 pkg	OETKER Vanilla Sugar	1 pkg.
250 mL	butter or margarine, cold	1 cup

Decoration:

250 mL	sifted icing sugar	1 cup
3 pkg	OETKER Vanilla Sugar	3 pkg.

Dough:

PREHEAT oven to 150°C (300°F). Grease a baking sheet.

BLEND flour, ground almonds, sugar and vanilla sugar together on a pastry board.

CUT cold butter into small pieces over dry ingredients. Work all ingredients together quickly to make a smooth dough.

ROLL a small amount at a time into pencil-like strips. Cut into small rolls about 5 cm (2″).

PLACE on prepared baking sheet. Shape into crescents.

BAKE at 150°C (300°F) for 10-15 min or until light golden.

ROLL warm cookies in mixture of icing sugar and vanilla sugar. Cool. Store in airtight container.

MAKES about 4 dozen.

*These cookies get better the longer they are kept.

Recipe No. 57

Nut Triangles

(Nussecken)

Topping:

175 mL	butter or margarine	¾ cup
150 mL	sugar	⅔ cup
1 pkg	OETKER Vanilla Sugar	1 pkg.
45 mL	water	3 tbsp.
1 btl	OETKER Rum Essence	1 btl.
750 mL	loosely packed ground walnuts, hazelnuts or pecans	3 cups

Pastry:

325 mL	all-purpose flour	1⅓ cups
10 mL	OETKER Baking Powder	2 tsp.
1	egg	1
1	egg yolk	1
125 mL	sugar	½ cup
1 pkg	OETKER Vanilla Sugar	1 pkg.
125 mL	butter or margarine, cold	½ cup

Filling:

50 mL	apricot or other jam	¼ cup

Decoration:

1 pkg	OETKER Chocofix OR semi-sweet chocolate, melted	1 pkg.

Topping:
COMBINE butter, sugar, vanilla sugar and water in saucepan. Bring to a boil. Stir in rum essence and nuts. Set aside to cool while preparing pastry.
Pastry:
PREHEAT oven to 150°C (300°F). Grease a 32 cm x 23 cm (13″ x 9″) cookie sheet.
SIFT flour and baking powder onto pastry board. Make a well in centre.
PUT egg, egg yolk, sugar and vanilla sugar in well. Work a little of flour into centre mixture.
CUT butter into small pieces. Quickly work all ingredients together into a smooth dough.
ROLL out dough on prepared cookie sheet.
SPREAD jam over dough. Spread cooled topping over jam.
BAKE on middle oven rack at 150°C (300°F) for 20-25 min or until golden.
PLACE pouch of Chocofix in boiling water to soften contents. Drizzle Chocofix or melted chocolate over baked dough.
CUT in triangles. Store in airtight container in cool place.
*Nut triangles improve if prepared several days before using.

Recipe No. 58

Coconut Wheels

(Kokosscheiben)

Cookie Dough:

250 mL	all-purpose flour	1 cup
10 mL	OETKER Baking Powder	2 tsp.
75 mL	sugar	⅓ cup
1 pkg	OETKER Vanilla Sugar	1 pkg.
2	egg yolks	2
3 drops	OETKER Lemon Essence	3 drops
125 mL	butter or margarine, cold	½ cup
500 mL	coconut	2 cups

Filling:

75 mL	apricot or raspberry jam or marmalade	⅓ cup
1 pkg	OETKER Chocofix, melted OR Chocolate Glaze II (Page 130)	1 pkg.

Decoration:

250 mL	sifted icing sugar	1 cup
2 pkg	OETKER Vanilla Sugar	2 pkg.

Dough:
PREHEAT oven to 150°C (300°F). Grease a baking sheet.
COMBINE flour, baking powder, sugar and vanilla sugar together on pastry board. Make a well in centre.
PUT egg and lemon essence in well. Work a little of dry ingredients into egg.
CUT butter into small pieces over flour mixture. Add coconut.
WORK all ingredients together quickly to make a smooth dough.
CHILL slightly for easy rolling (about ½ hour).
ROLL out dough on lightly floured surface to .5 cm (¼″) thickness.
CUT into 5 cm (2″) rounds. Place on prepared baking sheet.
BAKE at 150°C (300°F) for 15-20 min or until light golden. Cool.
SPREAD half of cookies with jam and remaining cookies with melted chocofix or chocolate glaze. Stick one of each cookie together.
ROLL in mixture of icing sugar and vanilla sugar.
MAKES about 2 dozen.

Recipe No. 59

Lemon Spritz Cookies

(Zitronen-Spritzgebaeck)

Cookie Dough:

300 mL	butter or margarine	1¼ cups
175 mL	sugar	¾ cup
1 pkg	OETKER Vanilla Sugar	1 pkg.
2	eggs	2
4 drops	OETKER Lemon Essence	4 drops
550 mL	all-purpose flour	2¼ cups
15 mL	*OETKER Baking Powder	1 tbsp.

*1 pkg. OETKER Baking Powder is equivalent to 15 mL or 1 tbsp.

Decoration:

chocolate chips, nuts or cherries

Dough:

PREHEAT oven to 160°C (325°F). Grease a baking sheet.
CREAM butter, sugar, vanilla sugar, eggs and lemon essence together until light and fluffy.
SIFT flour and baking powder together over creamed mixture. Mix well.
PRESS onto baking sheet using star tube in decorating bag.
PRESS chocolate chip, nut or cherry half into centre of cookies.
BAKE on middle oven rack at 160°C (325°F) for 10-15 min or until light golden. Cool slightly then remove from pan and cool completely. Store in airtight container.
MAKES about 9 dozen.

Recipe No. 60

Aniseed Wafers

(Anisboegen)

Batter:

4	eggs	4
175 mL	sugar	¾ cup
1 pkg	OETKER Vanilla Sugar	1 pkg.
175 mL	all-purpose flour	¾ cup
	aniseed	

Method:

PREHEAT oven to 180°C (350°F). Grease a baking sheet.
COMBINE eggs, sugar and vanilla sugar in small mixer bowl.
BEAT on high speed of electric mixer until thick and creamy.
FOLD in flour, gently but thoroughly.
DROP mixture by small spoonfuls onto prepared baking sheet, leaving about 4 cm (1½") between each for spreading.
SPRINKLE with aniseed.
BAKE on middle oven rack at 180°C (350°F) for 8-10 min or until lightly browned.
WHILE still hot, place each cookie over a wooden spoon handle to make the bent shape. Cool completely.
MAKES about 5 dozen.

Recipe No. 61

Chocolate Spritz Cookies

(Schokoladen-Spritzgebaeck)

Cookie Dough:

300 mL	butter or margarine	1¼ cups
175 mL	sugar	¾ cups
1 pkg	OETKER Vanilla Sugar	1 pkg.
1	egg white	1
500 mL	all-purpose flour	2 cups
10 mL	OETKER Baking Powder	2 tsp.
125 mL	ground almonds	½ cup
2 sq	semi-sweet chocolate, grated	2 sq.

Method:

PREHEAT oven to 160°C (325°F). Grease a baking sheet.
CREAM butter, sugar, vanilla sugar and egg white together.
SIFT flour and baking powder together over creamed mixture.
ADD almonds and grated chocolate. Fold all ingredients together until well blended.
PUT mixture into decorating bag with star tube.
Squeeze onto baking sheet in desired shapes OR drop onto sheet by small spoonfuls.
BAKE on middle oven rack at 160°C (325°F) for 10-15 min. Cool then remove from sheet. Store in airtight container.
MAKES about 9 dozen.

Recipe No. 62

Jelly Filled Doughnuts

(Faschingskrapfen)

Yeast Dough:

750 mL	all-purpose flour	3 cups
1 pkg	OETKER Active Dry Yeast	1 pkg.
75 mL	sugar	⅓ cup
1 pkg	OETKER Vanilla Sugar	1 pkg.
pinch	salt	pinch
45 mL	rum	3 tbsp.
½ btl	OETKER Lemon Essence	½ btl.
4	egg yolks	4
90 mL	butter or margarine, melted	6 tbsp.
250 mL	milk, lukewarm	1 cup

Filling:

250 mL	apricot jam (or your favourite kind)	1 cup
	oil or shortening for frying	

Decoration:

75 mL	sifted icing sugar	⅓ cup
1 pkg	OETKER Vanilla Sugar	1 pkg.

Yeast Dough:

COMBINE flour and yeast in large mixing bowl. Make a well in centre.
PUT sugar, vanilla sugar, salt, rum, lemon essence, egg yolks and melted butter in well.
WORK flour into centre ingredients, gradually adding milk to make a soft dough.
BEAT dough with wooden spoon or by hand until blistered and shiny in appearance.
LET RISE in warm place until doubled in size, about 1 hr.
BEAT down risen dough.
ROLL OUT on floured surface to .5 cm (¼″) thickness. Cut out with floured round cutter. For each doughnut, put a little jam on one round. Moisten edges of bottom of dough and place another round over jam. Press edges together to seal completely. Place on floured surface.
LET RISE until doubled in size, about 40 min.
HEAT deep fat to 190°C (375°F). Fry doughnuts, a few at a time, until golden brown. Turn to brown on other side.
REMOVE from fat. Drain on paper towelling.
COOL slightly then dip in mixture of icing sugar and vanilla sugar to coat well.

Recipe No. 63

Nut or Poppy Seed Crescents

(Nuss-oder Mohnbeugel)

Yeast Dough:

750 mL	all-purpose flour	3 cups
1 pkg	OETKER Active Dry Yeast	1 pkg.
150 mL	sifted icing sugar	⅔ cup
1 pkg	OETKER Vanilla Sugar	1 pkg.
pinch	salt	pinch
2	egg yolks	2
250 mL	butter or margarine, melted	1 cup
½ btl	OETKER Lemon Essence	½ btl.
125 mL	warm milk	½ cup

Nut Filling:

150 mL	sugar	⅔ cup
1 pkg	OETKER Vanilla Sugar	1 pkg.
50 mL	sweet (unsalted) butter	¼ cup
75 mL	milk	⅓ cup
550 mL	ground nuts (pecans, hazelnuts or walnuts)	2¼ cups
15 mL	rum	1 tbsp.
½ btl	OETKER Lemon Essence	½ btl.
pinch	cinnamon	pinch

Poppy Seed Filling:

150 mL	sugar	⅔ cup
1 pkg	OETKER Vanilla Sugar	1 pkg.
125 mL	milk	½ cup
15-30 mL	liquid honey	1-2 tbsp.
550 mL	ground poppy seeds	2¼ cups
1 btl	OETKER Lemon Essence	1 btl.
pinch	cinnamon	pinch

Glaze:

1	egg yolk	1
15 mL	milk	1 tbsp.

Yeast Dough:
PLACE ⅔ of flour in large mixing bowl. Stir in yeast. Make a well in centre.
PUT icing sugar, vanilla sugar, salt, egg yolks, melted butter and lemon essence in well.
WORK flour into centre, adding milk and remaining flour gradually.
KNEAD dough well until shiny and blistered in appearance.
LET RISE in warm place until doubled in size.
Meanwhile, prepare filling.

Nut Filling:
COMBINE sugar, vanilla sugar, butter and milk.
Bring to a boil, stirring constantly. Stir in nuts, rum, lemon essence and cinnamon. Cool.

Poppy Seed Filling:
COMBINE sugar, vanilla sugar, milk and honey.
Bring to a boil, stirring constantly. Stir in poppy seeds, essence and cinnamon. Cool.

Dough (continued):
PREHEAT oven to 180°C (350°F). Grease a baking sheet.
KNEAD well on floured board.
SHAPE dough into a roll. Cut in 4 cm (1½″) pieces. Roll each piece into an oval shape.
PLACE small amount of filling on dough. Fold 2 sides of dough over filling, sealing seam well. Shape into a crescent on prepared baking sheet.
BRUSH with mixture of egg yolk and milk.
BAKE on middle oven rack at 180°C (350°F) for 15-20 min or until golden.

Recipe No. 64

Yeast Dumplings

(Hefeknoedel)

Yeast Dough:

750 mL	all-purpose flour	3 cups
1 pkg	OETKER Active Dry Yeast	1 pkg.
pinch	salt	pinch
50 mL	sugar	¼ cup
125 mL	butter or margarine, melted	½ cup
2	eggs	2
15 mL	rum	1 tbsp.
1	grated rind of fresh lemon	1
250 mL	lukewarm milk	1 cup

Filling:

250 mL	plum jam or marmalade	1 cup

Decoration:

poppy seeds
sugar or nuts
melted butter

Yeast Dough:
COMBINE flour, yeast and salt in large mixing bowl. Make a well in centre.
PUT sugar, melted butter, eggs, rum and lemon rind in well.
MIX ingredients, working from centre and gradually adding milk.
BEAT dough until shiny and blistered.
LET RISE in warm place until doubled in size.
TURN out on floured board. Shape into a roll.
CUT into 2 cm (1″) pieces.
PLACE jam in middle of dough slice. Press sides together and shape into a ball enclosing filling completely.
LEAVE dough balls on floured board. Cover with a cloth.
LET RISE until doubled in size.
DROP dumplings into large pot of boiling salted water, turning once on each side.
LIFT out with slotted spoon. Drain well. Place in dessert dishes.
SPRINKLE with poppy seeds mixed with sugar or nuts. Drizzle with a little melted butter.

oetker
GERM

Recipe No. 65

Yeast Guglhupf

(Guglhupf)

Dough:

750 mL	all-purpose flour	3 cups
1 pkg	OETKER Active Dry Yeast	1 pkg.
125 mL	sugar	½ cup
1 pkg	OETKER Vanilla Sugar	1 pkg.
175 mL	butter, melted and cooled	¾ cup
5	egg yolks	5
1	egg	1
1 btl	OETKER Lemon Essence	1 btl.
1 btl	OETKER Rum Essence	1 btl.
250 mL	lukewarm milk	1 cup
500 mL	raisins	2 cups

Pan Coating:

45 mL	ground almonds	3 tbsp.
30 mL	fine dry bread crumbs	2 tbsp.

Decoration:

30 mL	sifted icing sugar	2 tbsp.
1 pkg	OETKER Vanilla Sugar	1 pkg.

Yeast Dough:

SIFT flour into large bowl.
ADD yeast, sugar, vanilla sugar, melted butter, egg yolks, egg, lemon and rum essence.
WORK dough together with your hands, adding warm milk as you mix. Continue working dough until it is shiny and leaves sides of bowl.
COVER with greased waxed paper and let rise in warm place until doubled in volume (about 2 hrs).
PREPARE PAN: Grease a 24 cm (9½″) fluted tube pan.
SPRINKLE with mixture of ground almonds and bread crumbs.
STIR down risen batter. Add raisins and mix well.
TURN batter into prepared pan and let rise in warm place until almost doubled (about 1 hr).
BAKE on lower oven rack at 180°C (350°F) for 50-60 min.
COOL 10 min then remove from pan. Cool completely.
SPRINKLE with mixture of icing sugar and vanilla sugar.

Recipe No. 66

Bear Claws

(Baerentatzen)

Dough:

125 mL	butter or margarine, cold	½ cup
400 mL	all-purpose flour	1⅔ cups
400 mL	cake and pastry flour	1⅔ cups
1 pkg	OETKER Active Dry Yeast	1 pkg.
125 mL	sugar	½ cup
1 pkg	OETKER Vanilla Sugar	1 pkg.
125 mL	lukewarm milk	½ cup
125 mL	butter or margarine, melted	½ cup
2	eggs	2
15 mL	rum	1 tbsp.
½ btl	OETKER Rum Essence	½ btl.

Filling:

125 mL	ground hazelnuts, walnuts or pecans	½ cup
125 mL	ground almonds	½ cup
125 mL	sugar	½ cup
1 pkg	OETKER Vanilla Sugar	1 pkg.
5 mL	cinnamon	1 tsp.

Glaze:

1	egg, beaten	1

Yeast Dough:

GRATE cold butter coarsely as you would cheese. Put in fridge.
PLACE half of flours in large bowl. Stir in yeast. Make a well in centre.
PLACE sugar, vanilla sugar, milk, melted butter, eggs, rum and rum essence in well.
WORK all ingredients together, beating until batter is shiny and blistered in appearance.
KNEAD in remaining flour until smooth.
ROLL dough to a rectangle 1 cm (½″) thick.
SPRINKLE half of grated butter in middle of dough. Fold left side of dough over butter. Sprinkle with rest of butter. Fold right side over.
FLATTEN dough a little with rolling pin. Roll out again to a rectangle 1 cm (½″) thick. Repeat folding. Chill dough 30 min.
REPEAT rolling and folding twice more with 30 min rest in between.

Filling:

COMBINE all ingredients.
ROLL out dough to 1 cm (½″) thickness. Cut into 8 cm (3″) squares. Reserve some filling.
SPRINKLE remaining filling on half of each square of dough.
FOLD dough in half, corner to corner to form a triangle. Press to seal seams.
CUT slits in longer side of dough. Brush with beaten egg and sprinkle with reserved filling. Shape dough to look like bear claws. Twist corner a little to centre so slits open slightly.
PLACE on greased baking sheet.
BAKE on middle oven rack at 180°C (350°F) for 12-20 min or until crisp and golden.

Recipe No. 67

Pizza

Dough:

500 mL	all-purpose flour	2 cups
1 pkg	OETKER Active Dry Yeast	1 pkg.
5 mL	salt	1 tsp.
125 mL	butter or margarine, melted	½ cup
50 mL	lukewarm water	¼ cup
30 mL	sour cream	2 tbsp.

Topping:

	olive or cooking oil	
200 g	bacon, diced	½ lb.
500 mL	diced, cooked ham	2 cups
200 g	mozzarella cheese slices	½ lb.
8	tomatoes, thinly sliced	8
12	stuffed olives, halved	12
	oregano, salt, pepper to taste	
	grated parmesan cheese	

Yeast Dough:
PREHEAT oven to 180°C (350°F).
COMBINE flour, yeast and salt in large bowl or on pastry board. Make a well in centre.
PUT melted butter, water and sour cream in well. Working from centre, stir until all ingredients are well blended. Knead until shiny and blistered in appearance. Divide dough into 4 equal portions.
ROLL out each portion on a greased baking sheet to a 25 cm (10″) circle.
BRUSH lightly with oil.
Topping:
DISTRIBUTE bacon, ham, cheese, tomatoes and olives evenly over dough.
SPRINKLE with seasonings and parmesan cheese.
BAKE on middle oven rack at 180°C (350°F) for 20-25 min or until crust is golden and filling is hot.

Recipe No. 68

Baked Ham & Cheese Perogies

(Russische Piroggen)

Dough:

500 mL	all-purpose flour	2 cups
1 pkg	OETKER Active Dry Yeast	1 pkg.
5 mL	salt	1 tsp.
125 mL	butter or margarine, melted	½ cup
50 mL	lukewarm milk	¼ cup
30 mL	sour cream	2 tbsp.

Filling:

375 mL	diced cooked ham	1½ cups
375 mL	shredded mozzarella cheese	1½ cups
	salt and pepper to taste	
1	egg, beaten	1

Glaze:

1	egg, beaten	1

Yeast Dough:
PREHEAT oven to 190°C (375°F). Grease a baking sheet.
COMBINE flour, yeast and salt in large bowl. Make a well in centre.
PUT melted butter, milk and sour cream in well.
WORK dry ingredients into centre ingredients until all ingredients are blended into a smooth, soft dough. Continue working dough until shiny and blistered in appearance.
ROLL out dough to 1 cm (½″) thickness. Cut into 8 cm (3″) rounds.
Filling:
COMBINE all filling ingredients. Mix well.
PLACE small amount of filling on each round of dough. Fold 2 sides over to meet in centre. Press to seal top seam.
BRUSH with beaten egg. Place on prepared baking sheet.
BAKE on middle oven rack at 190°C (375°F) for 15-20 min or until golden.
SERVE warm with soups, salads or wines.

Recipe No. 69

Savarin

Yeast Dough:

500 mL	all-purpose flour	2 cups
1 pkg	OETKER Active Dry Yeast	1 pkg.
45 mL	sugar	3 tbsp.
1 pkg	OETKER Vanilla Sugar	1 pkg.
1	egg	1
2	egg yolks	2
45 mL	melted butter	3 tbsp.
1 btl	OETKER Lemon Essence	1 btl.
125 mL	lukewarm milk	½ cup

Syrup:

125 mL	rum	½ cup
75 mL	cherry brandy or maraschino cherry juice	⅓ cup
60-75 mL	water	4-5 tbsp.
50 mL	sugar	¼ cup
1 pkg	OETKER Vanilla Sugar	1 pkg.

Decoration:

250 mL	whipping cream	1 cup
1 pkg	OETKER Whip-It	1 pkg.
30 mL	sifted icing sugar	2 tbsp.
1 pkg	OETKER Vanilla Sugar	1 pkg.
30 mL	red currant jam	2 tbsp.

Yeast Dough:
COMBINE flour and yeast in large mixing bowl. Make a well in centre.
PUT sugar, vanilla sugar, egg, egg yolks, melted butter and lemon essence in centre of well.
MIX ingredients, working from centre and gradually adding milk.
BEAT dough until it is shiny and blistered in appearance.
LET RISE in warm place for 30 min.
BEAT dough again until smooth.
TURN dough into greased and floured savarin mould.
LET RISE in warm place for 20 min.
BAKE on middle oven rack at 180°C (350°F) for 40-50 min or until toothpick inserted in centre comes out clean.
REMOVE from pan immediately.
Syrup:
COMBINE all ingredients in saucepan. Bring to a boil.
POUR hot syrup over cake, letting it soak in. Cool cake before decorating.
Decoration:
BEAT cream to soft peaks. Gradually add Whip-It, icing sugar and vanilla sugar, beating to stiff peaks. Pile cream mixture in centre of savarin ring. Decorate cream with jam.

Recipe No. 70

Steamed Dumplings with Vanilla Sauce

(Dampfnudeln)

Dough:

750 mL	all-purpose flour	3 cups
1 pkg	OETKER Active Dry Yeast	1 pkg.
75 mL	sugar	⅓ cup
1 pkg	OETKER Vanilla Sugar	1 pkg.
1	egg	1
2	egg yolks	2
125 mL	butter, melted	½ cup
375 mL	lukewarm milk	1½ cups

Glaze:

45 mL	melted butter for brushing	3 tbsp.
	milk	

Vanilla Sauce:

875 mL	milk	3½ cups
1 pkg	OETKER Vanilla Pudding and Pie Filling	1 pkg.
75 mL	sugar	⅓ cup
2 pkg	OETKER Vanilla Sugar	2 pkg.

Yeast Dough:
SIFT flour into large bowl. Stir in yeast. Make a well in centre.
PUT sugar, vanilla sugar, egg, egg yolks and melted butter in well.
MIX ingredients, working from centre and gradually adding milk.
BEAT dough until it has a shiny, blistered appearance.
LET RISE in warm place until doubled in size.
TURN out on floured board. Shape into a roll or ball.
CUT into 4 cm (1½") doughnut shaped pieces.
PLACE dough pieces 5 cm (2") apart in baking dish. Brush with melted butter.
POUR a little milk in bottom of pan.
LET RISE in warm place until doubled in size.
BAKE on middle oven rack at 180°C (350°F) for 40-50 min or until golden.
Sauce:
COMBINE 125 mL (½ cup) milk, pudding and pie filling, sugar and vanilla sugar.
HEAT remaining 750 mL (3 cups) milk to boiling. Stir in pudding mixture.
BRING to boil again, stirring constantly. Cool, stirring occasionally.
PLACE dumplings in serving dish or individual dishes. Pour sauce over dumplings.

Recipe No. 71

Fruit Cream Puffs

(Fruchtcreme-Krapferl)

Batter:

250 mL	water	1 cup
125 mL	shortening or lard	½ cup
250 mL	all-purpose flour	1 cup
1 mL	salt	¼ tsp.
4	eggs	4

Glaze:

400 mL	sifted icing sugar	1⅔ cups
1 btl	OETKER Lemon Essence	1 btl.
15-30 mL	hot water	1-2 tbsp.

Filling:

300 mL	cold milk	1¼ cups
1 pkg	OETKER Strawberry Mousse	1 pkg.

Decoration:

strawberries or raspberries

Batter:

PREHEAT oven to 200°C (400°F). Grease a baking sheet.

COMBINE water and shortening in saucepan. Bring to a boil.

ADD flour and salt all at once. Cook, stirring vigorously until mixture leaves sides of pan, about 1 min.

TURN into mixing bowl and let cool.

ADD eggs, 1 at a time, beating well after each addition until smooth and shiny.

DROP batter by spoonfuls in 5 cm (2″) rounds onto prepared baking sheet. Make small well in centre of each.

BAKE at 200°C (400°F) for 15 min then reduce heat to 180°C (350°F) and bake 25-30 min longer or until crisp and golden. Cool. Cut in half horizontally.

Glaze:

COMBINE icing sugar, lemon essence and enough hot water to make a smooth glaze of paste-like consistency.

SPREAD glaze over top of puffs.

Filling:

PREPARE Strawberry Mousse with milk according to package directions.

FILL bottom of puffs with filling. Place glazed top over filling.

DECORATE with strawberries or raspberries.

Recipe No. 72 (Picture Page 103)

Eclairs

Batter:

250 mL	water	1 cup
pinch	salt	pinch
125 mL	shortening	½ cup
250 mL	all-purpose flour	1 cup
4	eggs	4

Filling No. 1:

red currant jam
Vanilla Cream (Page 126)

OR

Filling No. 2:

500 mL	whipping cream	2 cups
2 pkg	OETKER Whip-It	2 pkg.
45 mL	sifted icing sugar	3 tbsp.
2 pkg	OETKER Vanilla Sugar	2 pkg.

Glaze:

1 pkg	OETKER Chocofix OR Chocolate Glaze II (Page 130)	1 pkg

Batter:
PREHEAT oven to 200°C (400°F). Grease a baking sheet.
COMBINE water, salt and shortening in saucepan. Bring to a boil.
ADD flour all at once. Cook stirring vigorously until dough leaves sides of pan and forms a ball, about 1 min.
TURN batter into a mixing bowl. Cool slightly.
BEAT in eggs, 1 at a time, beating well after each addition until smooth.
PLACE dough in decorating bag with large round tube.
PRESS two finger-like strips beside each other on prepared baking sheet then press a third strip on top.
BAKE on middle oven rack at 200°C (400°F) for 15 min then reduce heat to 180°C (350°F) and bake 30-35 min longer or until crisp and golden. Cool and cut lengthwise.
FILLING (Use No. 1 OR No. 2)
No. 1 SPREAD small amount of jam on bottom of eclairs.
SPREAD a generous amount of Vanilla Cream over jam.
No. 2 BEAT cream to soft peaks. Add Whip-It, icing sugar and vanilla sugar, gradually beating to stiff peaks.
SPREAD generous amount of cream filling on bottom of eclairs.
Glaze:
PREPARE Chocofix according to package directions or Chocolate Glaze. Spread over top of eclairs. Place glazed tops over filling.

Recipe No. 73 (Picture Page 107)

Mocha Ring

(Mokkakranz)

Batter:

125 mL	water	½ cup
30 mL	butter or margarine	2 tbsp.
150 mL	all-purpose flour	⅔ cup
2-3	eggs	2-3
2 mL	OETKER Baking Powder	½ tsp.

Glaze:

325 mL	sifted icing sugar	1-⅓ cups
30-45 mL	hot strong coffee	2-3 tbsp.
	OR	
	Coffee Glaze (Page 130)	

Filling:

250 mL	whipping cream	1 cup
1 pkg	OETKER Whip-It	1 pkg.
1 pkg	OETKER Vanilla Sugar	1 pkg.
15 mL	sifted icing sugar	1 tbsp.
10 mL	instant coffee powder	2 tsp.
	OR USE:	
	Coffee Cream Filling I (Page 127)	
15-30 mL	rum	1-2 tbsp.
1 btl	OETKER Rum Essence	1 btl.

Batter:

PREHEAT oven to 200°C (400°F). Grease and flour a baking sheet.

COMBINE water and butter in saucepan. Bring to a boil.

ADD flour all at once. Cook, stirring vigorously until mixture forms a smooth ball and leaves sides of pan, about 1 min.

TURN into mixing bowl. Cool slightly.

ADD eggs, 1 at a time, beating well after each addition until smooth and shiny. Cool.

STIR in baking powder. Put batter in decorating bag with large tube. Squeeze batter onto prepared baking sheet in a 16 cm (6½″) circle. Make another ring beside first one then another on top in between first two.

BAKE on middle oven rack at 200°C (400°F) for 30-35 min or until crisp and golden. Cool.

SLICE ring in half horizontally to make 2 layers.

Glaze:

COMBINE icing sugar and enough hot coffee to make a smooth glaze of paste-like consistency OR prepare Coffee Glaze.

SPREAD glaze over top of ring.

Filling:

BEAT whipping cream just until it starts to stiffen.

ADD Whip-It, vanilla sugar, icing sugar and coffee, beating to stiff peaks.

OR Prepare Coffee Cream Filling I.

FOLD rum and essence into filling.

FILL bottom of pastry ring with filling. Cover with glazed pastry top.

Recipe No. 74

Chocolate Glazed Doughnuts

(Kapuziner-Krapferl)

Batter:

175 mL	milk	¾ cup
50 mL	butter or margarine	¼ cup
1 pkg	OETKER Vanilla Sugar	1 pkg.
150 mL	all-purpose flour	⅔ cup
3	eggs	3
2 mL	OETKER Baking Powder	½ tsp.
	oil, shortening or lard for frying	

Decoration:

5 sq	semi-sweet chocolate, grated	5 sq.
	whipping cream	
	red currant jam or jelly	

Batter:

COMBINE milk, butter and vanilla sugar in saucepan. Bring to a boil.

ADD flour all at once. Cook, stirring vigorously until mixture forms a smooth ball and leaves sides of pan, about 1 min.

TURN into mixing bowl. Cool slightly.

ADD eggs, one at a time, beating well after each addition until smooth and shiny. Cool.

STIR in baking powder.

HEAT oil in deep fryer to 190°C (375°F).

DROP batter by spoonfuls into hot oil, a few at a time.

BROWN on one side, then turn to brown on all sides.

LIFT out with slotted spoon. Drain on paper towelling.

ROLL doughnuts in grated chocolate.

WHIP cream to stiff peaks. Decorate doughnuts with cream and drizzle with jam.

Recipe No. 75

Cheese Knots

(Pikante kleine Baeckerei)

Dough:

500 mL	all-purpose flour	2 cups
175 mL	OETKER/GUSTIN Corn Starch	⅔ cup
5 mL	OETKER Baking Powder	1 tsp.
pinch	salt	pinch
pinch	pepper	pinch
pinch	paprika	pinch
1	egg	1
1	egg white	1
½	egg yolk	½
30 mL	sour cream	2 tbsp.
325 mL	grated cheese	1⅓ cups
250 mL	butter or margarine, cold	1 cup

Glaze:

½	egg yolk	½
30 mL	milk	2 tbsp.

Decoration:

caraway seeds, poppy seeds, or sesame seeds

Dough:

PREHEAT oven to 180°C (350°F). Grease a baking sheet.

COMBINE flour, corn starch, baking powder, salt, pepper and paprika on pastry board. Make a well in centre.

PUT egg, egg white, ½ egg yolk and sour cream into well. Work a little flour into egg mixture. Add grated cheese.

CUT cold butter into small pieces over flour mixture.

WORK all ingredients together quickly to make a smooth dough.

SHAPE dough into pencil-like rolls and twist like a knot. Place on prepared baking sheet. Brush with mixture of glaze ingredients. Sprinkle with seeds.

BAKE on middle oven rack at 180°C (350°F) for 8-15 min or until golden.

MAKES about 8 dozen.

Recipe No. 76

Cheese Rings

(Gespritzte Kaeseringe)

Ingredients:

125 mL	butter or margarine	½ cup
200 mL	grated Gouda cheese	¾ cup
175 mL	all-purpose flour	⅔ cup
1 mL	OETKER Baking Powder	¼ tsp.
pinch	paprika	pinch

Pastry:

PREHEAT oven to 180°C (350°F). Grease a baking sheet.

CREAM butter and cheese together. Gradually add flour, baking powder and paprika. Mix well.

PUT dough in decorating bag with star tube. Squeeze onto prepared baking sheet in small circles.

OR Drop mixture by spoonfuls onto sheet. Flatten slightly with floured fork.

BAKE on middle oven rack at 180°C (350°F) for 10-15 min or until light golden.

MAKES about 2 dozen.

Recipe No. 77

Cheese Clovers

(Garnierte Salzbaeckerei)

Pastry:

550 mL	all-purpose flour	2¼ cups
15 mL	*OETKER Baking Powder	1 tbsp.
3	egg yolks	3
125 mL	sour cream	½ cup
250 mL	butter or margarine, cold	1 cup

*1 pkg. OETKER Baking Powder is equivalent to 15 mL or 1 tbsp.

Filling:

1 pkg	(250 g/8 oz.) Gervais or ricotta cheese	1 pkg.
90 mL	sour cream	6 tbsp.
30 mL	finely chopped green onions, optional	2 tbsp.
	salt and pepper to taste	

Decoration:

sliced olives
paprika

Pastry:
PREHEAT oven to 180°C (350°F). Grease baking sheet.
SIFT flour and baking powder onto pastry board. Make a well in centre.
PUT egg yolks and sour cream in well. Work a little flour into egg mixture.
CUT cold butter into small pieces over flour mixture.
WORK all ingredients together quickly to make a smooth dough.
ROLL out dough on floured surface to .5 cm (¼″) thickness.
CUT out shapes with floured cutter. Place on prepared baking sheet.
BAKE on middle oven rack at 180° (350°F) for 10-15 min until light golden. Cool.

Filling:
COMBINE all filling ingredients. Beat well until smooth. Put into decorating bag with large star tube.
DECORATE each pastry with a rosette of filling. Garnish with olive and sprinkle with paprika.

Recipe No. 78

Parmesan Crescents

(Parmesan Kipferl)

Ingredients:

150 mL	all-purpose flour	⅔ cup
10 mL	OETKER Baking Powder	2 tsp.
175 mL	grated Parmesan cheese	¾ cup
1	egg	1
125 mL	butter or margarine, cold	½ cup

Pastry:
PREHEAT oven to 180°C (350°F). Grease a baking sheet.
SIFT flour and baking powder together onto pastry board. Make a well in centre.
PLACE cheese and egg in well. Work a little flour into egg mixture.
CUT cold butter into small pieces over flour mixture. Work all ingredients together quickly into a smooth dough.
SHAPE dough into rolls about the size of a pencil.
CUT into 5 cm (2″) pieces. Form into crescents on prepared baking sheet.
BAKE on middle oven rack at 180°C (350°F) for 10-15 min or until golden. Cool.
MAKES about 5½ dozen crescents.

Recipe No. 79

Cheese Sticks

(Kaesestangen)

Pastry Dough:

325 mL	all-purpose flour	1⅓ cups
15 mL	*OETKER Baking Powder	1 tbsp.
250 mL	butter or margarine, cold	1 cup
1	egg	1
1	egg white	1
375 mL	grated cheese	1½ cups

*1 pkg. OETKER Baking Powder is the equivalent of 15 mL or 1 tbsp.

Decoration:

1	egg yolk, beaten	1
15 mL	milk	1 tbsp.
	caraway seeds, poppy seeds or sesame seeds	

Pastry:

PREHEAT oven to 180°C (350°F). Grease a baking sheet.
COMBINE flour and baking powder on pastry board. Make a well in centre.
PUT egg and egg white into well. Work a little flour into eggs.
CUT cold butter into small pieces over dough.
WORK quickly into a smooth dough, adding cheese as you mix.
CHILL dough 30 min.
ROLL out thinly on floured board. Cut into 8 cm x 1 cm (3″ x ½″) strips.
BRUSH with mixture of egg yolk and milk. Sprinkle with seeds.
BAKE on middle rack at 180°C (350°F) for 10-15 min or until golden.
MAKES about 10 dozen.

Recipe No. 80

Cheese Rounds

(Kaesekrapferl)

Pastry Dough:

250 mL	all-purpose flour	1 cup
5 mL	OETKER Baking Powder	1 tsp.
pinch	salt	pinch
300 mL	grated cheese	1¼ cups
30 mL	sour cream	2 tbsp.
175 mL	butter or margarine, cold	¾ cup

Glaze:

1	egg, beaten	1

Decoration:

caraway seeds, sesame seeds, or poppy seeds

Pastry:

PREHEAT oven to 160°C (325°F). Grease a baking sheet.
COMBINE flour, baking powder and salt on pastry board. Make a well in centre.
PUT cheese and sour cream in well. Mix a little flour into centre.
CUT butter in small pieces over flour mixture.
WORK all ingredients together quickly to form a smooth dough.
CHILL 1 hr for easy rolling.
ROLL out on floured board to .5 cm (¼″) thickness.
CUT into 4 cm (1½″) rounds.
BRUSH with beaten egg. Sprinkle with seeds. Place on prepared baking sheet.
BAKE on middle oven rack at 160°C (325°F) for 10-15 min or until golden.
MAKES about 3 dozen.

Recipe No. 81

Ham & Cheese Turnovers

(Schinkenzipferl)

Pastry Dough:

425 mL	all-purpose flour	1¾ cups
10 mL	OETKER Baking Powder	2 tsp.
2 mL	salt	½ tsp.
300 mL	dry cottage cheese, strained or ricotta	1¼ cups
250 mL	butter or margarine, cold	1 cup

Filling:

500 mL	diced ham	2 cups
125 mL	smoked cheese, grated	½ cup
45 mL	sour cream	3 tbsp.
	salt and pepper to taste	

Glaze:

1	egg yolk	1
10 mL	milk	2 tsp.

Pastry:
SIFT flour, baking powder and salt together onto pastry board. Make a well in centre.
PUT cheese in well. Cut butter into small pieces and place over cheese.
WORK all ingredients together quickly to form a smooth dough.
ROLL out dough on floured surface to .5 cm (¼″) thickness.
FOLD dough from right side to centre and then left side to centre. Fold sides together. Roll out again.
REPEAT folding and rolling 3 times more.
CHILL ½ hr for easy rolling when necessary.
MEANWHILE prepare filling. Combine all ingredients. Mix well.
CUT dough into 8 cm (3″) squares. Place small amount of filling on each square. Fold dough in half, corner to corner, to form a triangle. Press seams to seal well. Place on baking sheet lined with aluminum foil.
BRUSH with mixture of egg yolk and milk.
BAKE on middle oven rack at 180°C (350°F) for 25-30 min or until golden.

Recipe No. 82

Sausage Rolls

(Pasteten-Wuerstchen)

Filling:

3	strips of bacon, diced	3
125 mL	chopped onion	½ cup
350 g	package of lean sausage	12 oz.
1	egg	1
	salt and pepper to taste	
	curry and paprika	

Pastry Dough:

400 mL	all-purpose flour	1⅔ cups
15 mL	*OETKER Baking Powder	1 tbsp.
175 mL	dry cottage cheese, strained	¾ cup
175 mL	butter or margarine	¾ cup

*1 pkg. OETKER Baking Powder is equivalent to 15 mL or 1 tbsp.

Glaze

1	egg white	1
1	egg yolk, beaten	1
10 mL	milk	2 tsp.

Filling:
PREPARE filling before the pastry.
SAUTE bacon and onion together until tender.
REMOVE skin from sausage. Add to bacon mixture with egg and seasonings. Cook, stirring occasionally just until sausage loses its pink colour. Set aside.
Pastry:
PREHEAT oven to 180°C (350°F). Grease a baking sheet.
COMBINE flour and baking powder on pastry board. Make a well in centre. Put cheese in well.
CUT butter into small pieces over cheese.
WORK all ingredients together quickly to form a smooth dough.
ROLL out dough on floured board to .5 cm (¼″) thickness.
CUT dough into 12 cm x 10 cm (5″ x 4″) rectangles.
BRUSH with lightly beaten egg white to prevent pastry from getting soggy.
PLACE filling on pastry. Wrap pastry around filling. Seal edges well. Use any leftover pastry for decoration.
PLACE on prepared baking sheet. Brush with mixture of egg yolk and milk.
BAKE on middle oven rack at 180°C (350°F) for 25-35 min or until golden.

Recipe No. 83

Steamed Chocolate Cake with Chocolate Glaze

(Mohr im Hemd)

Batter:

125 mL	butter or margaine	½ cup
175 mL	sugar	¾ cup
1 pkg	OETKER Vanilla Sugar	1 pkg.
5	egg yolks	5
4 sq	semi-sweet chocolate, melted	4 sq.
1 btl	OETKER Rum Essence	1 btl.
5	egg whites	5
325 mL	walnuts or pecans, chopped	1⅓ cups
75 mL	dry bread crumbs	⅓ cup
50 mL	all-purpose flour	¼ cup
1 mL	cinnamon	¼ tsp.

Glaze:

1 pkg	OETKER Chocofix OR Chocolate Glaze II (Page 130)	1 pkg.

Decoration:

whipped cream, optional

Batter:
GREASE and sprinkle with bread crumbs a 23 cm (9″) bundt or fluted tube pan.
CREAM butter, sugar, vanilla sugar, egg yolks, melted chocolate and rum essence together thoroughly, beating until thick and creamy.
BEAT egg whites to stiff but moist peaks.
ADD nuts, bread crumbs, flour and cinnamon to creamed mixture.
Stir well to blend.
FOLD in egg whites gently.
TURN into prepared pan filling ¾ full.
SET on rack in steamer or large saucepan. Fill with boiling water to halfway up cake pan.
COVER steamer with tight-fitting lid. Keep water boiling over low heat for 30-40 min.
Remove from steamer. Let stand 5 min then unmould. Cool.

Glaze:
PLACE pouch of Chocofix in boiling water to soften contents. OR Prepare Chocolate Glaze II. Pour over cooled cake.
DECORATE base with whipped cream if desired.

Recipe No. 84

Crêpes "Parisienne"

Batter:

250 mL	all-purpose flour	1 cup
2 mL	OETKER Baking Powder	½ tsp.
30 mL	icing sugar	2 tbsp.
1 pkg	OETKER Vanilla Sugar	1 pkg.
pinch	salt	pinch
2	eggs	2
250 mL	milk	1 cup
15 mL	melted butter	1 tbsp.

Filling:

1 pkg	OETKER Chocofix	1 pkg.
30 mL	whipping cream	2 tbsp.
5 drops	OETKER Rum Essence	5 drops
125 mL	ground hazelnuts, walnuts or pecans	½ cup
30 mL	sugar	2 tbsp.

Decoration:

125 mL	whipping cream	½ cup
½ pkg	OETKER Whip-It	½ pkg.
30 mL	sifted icing sugar	2 tbsp.
1 pkg	OETKER Vanilla Sugar	1 pkg.

Batter:
SIFT flour, baking powder, icing sugar, vanilla sugar and salt into mixing bowl.
ADD eggs, milk and melted butter.
BEAT well to make a smooth thin batter.
PREHEAT 15 cm (6″) frying pan or crêpe pan. Grease lightly with butter.
POUR about 30 mL (2 tbsp.) batter into hot pan. Tilt pan to cover bottom with thin layer of batter. When lightly browned, turn to brown other side. Repeat with remaining batter. Turn out on baking sheet. Keep warm in very low oven.

Filling:
HEAT Chocofix, over low heat until soft. Stir in cream and rum essence.
BRING to a boil, stirring constantly.
SPREAD chocolate mixture over each crêpe. Fold into half then half again to form a triangle.
SPRINKLE with mixture of nuts and sugar.

Decoration:
BEAT cream to soft peaks. Gradually add Whip-It, icing sugar and vanilla sugar, beating to stiff peaks.
ARRANGE crêpes on serving plate. Decorate with whipped cream.

Recipe No. 85

Vanilla Mousse with Fruit

(Mousse mit Fruechten)

Ingredients:

1 pkg	OETKER Vanilla Mousse	1 pkg.
300 mL	cold milk	1¼ cups
45 mL	sugar	3 tbsp.
1	banana	1
2	oranges	2
1	apple	1

Decoration:

maraschino cherries, nuts, whipped cream, etc.

Method:

COMBINE mousse with milk. Prepare according to package directions. Stir in sugar.
PEEL fruits and cut into small pieces. Fold into mousse.
SPOON into dessert dishes. Decorate with maraschino cherry or as desired.

Recipe No. 86

Creamy Apples

(Geduenstete Aepfel)

Ingredients:

1 kg	apples	2 lb.
250 mL	white wine	1 cup
50 mL	sugar	¼ cup
30 mL	lemon juice	2 tbsp.

Filling:

50 mL	chopped nuts	¼ cup
50 mL	raisins	¼ cup
50 mL	jam or marmalade	¼ cup
pinch	cinnamon	pinch

Sauce:

1 pkg	OETKER Vanilla Pudding and Pie Filling	1 pkg.
875 mL	milk	3½ cups
125 mL	sugar	½ cup
30 mL	rum	2 tbsp.

Decoration:

maraschino cherries, jam, or chopped nuts, etc.

Method:

PEEL and core apples.
COMBINE wine, sugar and lemon juice in small saucepan. Bring to a boil. Place apples in liquid. Simmer until apples are tender but still hold their shape. Remove to serving plate.
COMBINE all filling ingredients. Stuff into apples.
PREPARE pudding and pie filling with milk according to package directions using 125 mL (½ cup) sugar. Add rum. Pour over apples.
DECORATE with cherries, jam or nuts.

Recipe No. 87

Meringue Surprise

Batter:

2	eggs	2
50 mL	sugar	¼ cup
1 pkg	OETKER Vanilla Sugar	1 pkg.
60 mL	all-purpose flour	4 tbsp.

Filling:

jam or marmalade

Topping:

1 pkg	OETKER Vanilla Pudding and Pie Filling	1 pkg.
75 mL	sugar	⅓ cup
625 mL	milk	2½ cups
1 btl	OETKER Rum Essence	1 btl.

Meringue:

3	egg whites	3
325 mL	sifted icing sugar	1⅓ cups

Decoration:

jam or marmalade

Batter:

PREHEAT oven to 180°C (350°F). Grease a 2L (39 cm x 26 cm/15″ x 10″) jelly roll pan. Line with waxed paper and grease again.
COMBINE eggs, sugar and vanilla sugar in mixing bowl. Beat at high speed of electric mixer until thick and creamy.
SIFT flour over egg mixture. Fold in gently.
SPREAD batter 1 cm (½″) thick in prepared pan.
BAKE on middle oven rack at 180°C (350°F) for 8-10 min or until toothpick inserted in centre comes out clean.
TURN out immediately onto waxed paper sprinkled with sugar. Rub back of paper with cold wet cloth to remove paper easily. Cool. Cut into 8 cm (3″) rounds.
DRIZZLE rum or spread jam over cakes.

Topping

COOK pudding and pie filling, sugar and milk according to package directions. Stir in rum essence. Pour into small mould 6 cm (2½″) in diameter. Chill until firm. Unmould onto cake rounds.

Meringue:

PREHEAT oven to 200°C (400°F).
BEAT egg whites to stiff but moist peaks. Gradually add icing sugar, beating to stiff peaks.
PUT meringue into decorating bag with star tube. Decorate puddings with meringue.
BAKE at 200°C (400°F) for 5-10 min or until golden.
DECORATE with jam.

Recipe No. 88

Almond Cream

(Mandelcreme)

Ingredients:

30 mL	sweet (unsalted) butter	2 tbsp.
30 mL	sugar	2 tbsp.
125 mL	chopped almonds	½ cup
1 pkg	OETKER Butterscotch Mousse	1 pkg.
300 mL	cold milk	1¼ cups

Decoration:

maraschino cherries, optional

Method:

COOK butter and sugar together in small saucepan, stirring constantly until golden.

ADD almonds. Cook until almonds are lightly roasted and coated with caramel. Pour onto buttered baking sheet and let cool. Process in food processor or smash in plastic bag to small pieces.

COMBINE mousse with milk. Prepare according to package directions. Stir in ¾ of crushed carmelized almonds.

SPOON into dessert dishes. Sprinkle with remaining carmelized almonds. Garnish with maraschino cherries if desired.

Recipe No. 89

Black & White Cream Parfait

(Schwarz-Weiss Creme)

Chocolate Layer:

1 pkg	OETKER Chocolate Pudding and Pie Filling	1 pkg.
625 mL	milk	2½ cups
50 mL	sugar	¼ cup

Cream Layer:

250 mL	whipping cream	1 cup
1 pkg	OETKER Whip-It	1 pkg.
45 mL	sifted icing sugar	3 tbsp.
1 pkg	OETKER Vanilla Sugar	1 pkg.
125 mL	chopped hazelnuts	½ cup

Method:

COMBINE pudding and pie filling with milk. Prepare according to package directions using 50 mL (¼ cup) sugar.

BEAT cream to soft peaks. Gradually add Whip-It, icing sugar and vanilla sugar beating to stiff peaks.

FOLD in ¾ of nuts.

In tall glasses, alternate layers of chocolate pudding and cream mixture, ending with cream. Sprinkle with remaining nuts.

Recipe No. 90

Raspberry Delight

(Himbeer-Dessert)

Pudding:

1 pkg	OETKER Raspberry Pudding and Pie Filling	1 pkg.
625 mL	milk	2½ cups
50 mL	sugar	¼ cup
50 mL	raspberry brandy or other liqueur	¼ cup

Sauce:

1 pkg	frozen raspberries	1 pkg.
15 mL	raspberry brandy or other liqueur	1 tbsp.

Decoration:

125 mL	whipping cream	½ cup
½ pkg	OETKER Whip-It	½ pkg.
15 mL	icing sugar	1 tbsp.
1 pkg	OETKER Vanilla Sugar	1 pkg.

Method:

COMBINE pudding and pie filling with milk. Prepare according to package directions using 50 mL (¼ cup) sugar. Stir in brandy.

TURN into individual moulds rinsed with cold water. Chill until cold.

HEAT raspberries and brandy together in small saucepan until heated through.

BEAT cream to soft peaks. Gradually add Whip-It, icing sugar and vanilla sugar, beating to stiff peaks.

UNMOULD puddings onto small plates. Spoon hot sauce over pudding. Decorate with whipped cream.

Recipe No. 91

Fruited Chocolate Rum Mousse

(Creme "Istanbul")

Ingredients:

175 mL	dried figs, chopped	¾ cup
125 mL	raisins	½ cup
30 mL	brandy	2 tbsp.
1 pkg	OETKER Chocolate Mousse	1 pkg.
300 mL	milk	1¼ cups
½ btl	OETKER Rum Essence	½ btl.
	whipped cream, optional	
	grated chocolate, optional	

Method:

CHOP figs and raisins into small pieces. Stir in brandy.

COMBINE mousse with milk. Prepare according to package directions. Stir in rum essence.

FOLD in figs and raisins.

SPOON into dessert dishes. Chill.

DECORATE with whipped cream and grated chocolate if desired.

Recipe No. 92

Russian Tea Cream

(Russiche Teecreme)

Ingredients:

1 pkg	OETKER Vanilla Mousse	1 pkg.
250 mL	cold milk	1 cup
75 mL	strong, black tea, cold	⅓ cup
30 mL	rum	2 tbsp.

Decoration:

*125 mL	drained fruit cocktail	½ cup
30 mL	rum, optional	2 tbsp.
	whipped cream	

*Use any fruits of your choice.

Method:

COMBINE mousse, milk and tea. Prepare according to package directions. Stir in rum.

SPOON into dessert dishes.

COMBINE drained fruit and 30 mL (2 tbsp.) rum if desired. (This can be mixed and left overnight for a more mellow flavour.)

SPOON fruit over mousse.

DECORATE with whipped cream.

Recipe No. 93

Irish Dessert

Ingredients:

1 pkg	OETKER Butterscotch Mousse	1 pkg.
300 mL	cold milk	1¼ cups
5 mL	instant coffee powder	1 tsp.
45 mL	rye whiskey	3 tbsp.
2 sq	semi-sweet chocolate, grated	2 sq.

Method:

COMBINE mousse and milk. Prepare according to package directions. Stir in coffee and rye.

BEAT until thick and creamy.

RESERVE a little chocolate for garnish. Fold remaining chocolate into mousse.

SPOON into dessert dishes. Sprinkle top with reserved chocolate. Cool before serving.

Vanilla Cream

(Vanillecreme)

Ingredients:

1 pkg	OETKER Vanilla Pudding and Pie Filling	1 pkg.
175 mL	sugar	¾ cup
625 mL	milk	2½ cups
250 mL	sweet (unsalted) butter	1 cup

Method:

COMBINE pudding and pie filling, sugar and 125 mL (½ cup) milk. Stir until smoothly blended.
RINSE saucepan with cold water.
HEAT remaining 500 mL (2 cups) milk to boiling. Stir in pudding mixture. Bring to a boil, stirring constantly.
REMOVE from heat. Cool to room temperature, stirring occasionally.
CREAM butter. Beat in pudding 15 mL(1 tbsp) at a time. (Butter and pudding must be at same temperature to prevent curdling.)

NOTE: Pudding can be cooked easily in microwave.

Chocolate Cream I

(Schokoladencreme I)

Ingredients:

1 pkg	OETKER Chocolate Pudding and Pie Filling	1 pkg.
125 mL	sugar	½ cup
625 mL	milk	2½ cups
300 mL	sweet (unsalted) butter	1¼ cups
3-4 sq	semi-sweet chocolate, melted and cooled	3-4 sq.

Method:

COMBINE pudding and pie filling, sugar and 125 mL (½ cup) milk. Stir until smoothly blended.
RINSE saucepan with cold water.
HEAT remaining 500 mL (2 cups) milk to boiling. Stir in pudding mixture. Bring to boil again, stirring constantly.
REMOVE from heat. Cool to room temperature, stirring occasionally.
CREAM butter. Beat in pudding and chocolate 15 mL (1 tbsp.) at a time. (Butter, chocolate and pudding must be at same temperature to prevent curdling.)

NOTE: Pudding can be cooked easily in microwave.

Chocolate Cream II

(Schokoladencreme II)

Ingredients:

375 mL	milk	1½ cups
1 pkg	OETKER Chocolate Frosting Mix	1 pkg.
325 mL	sweet (unsalted) butter	1⅓ cups
325 mL	sifted icing sugar	1⅓ cups
50 mL	sifted cocoa	¼ cup
1 btl	OETKER Rum Essence	1 btl.

Method:

* Have milk and butter at room temperature.
COMBINE milk and frosting mix in small mixer bowl. Beat at high speed of electric mixer until stiff peaks form, about 4 min.
LET SIT at room temperature for 15 min.
CREAM butter. Add chocolate frosting mixture, a spoonful at a time, beating until well blended. Gradually add icing sugar, cocoa and rum essence, beating until smooth and creamy.

Coffee Cream Filling I

(Kaffeecreme I)

Ingredients:

1 pkg	OETKER Vanilla Pudding and Pie Filling	1 pkg.
175 mL	sugar	¾ cup
500 mL	cold strong coffee	2 cups
125 mL	whipping cream	½ cup
250 mL	sweet (unsalted) butter	1 cup

Method:

COMBINE pudding and pie filling, sugar and 125 mL (½ cup) coffee. Stir until smoothly blended.
RINSE saucepan with cold water.
HEAT remaining 375 mL (1½ cups) coffee and whipping cream to boiling. Stir in pudding mixture. Bring to boil again, stirring constantly.
REMOVE from heat. Cool to room temperature, stirring occasionally.
CREAM butter. Beat in pudding 15 mL(1 tbsp) at a time. (Butter and pudding must be at same temperature to prevent curdling.)

Coffee Cream Filling II

(Kaffeecreme II)

Ingredients:

175 mL	strong black coffee	¾ cup
175 mL	milk	¾ cup
1 pkg	OETKER Coffee Frosting Mix	1 pkg.
325 mL	sweet (unsalted) butter	1¾ cups
250 mL	sifted icing sugar	1 cup

Method:

* Have coffee, milk and butter at room temperature.
COMBINE coffee, milk and frosting mix in small mixer bowl. Beat on high speed of electric mixer until stiff peaks form, about 4 min.
LET SIT at room temperature for 15 min.
CREAM butter. Gradually add icing sugar and frosting mixture, a spoonful at a time, beating until smooth and creamy.

Nut Cream (Pecan or Hazelnut)

(Nuss-oder Haselnusscreme)

Ingredients:

1 pkg	OETKER Vanilla Pudding and Pie Filling	1 pkg.
175 mL	sugar	¾ cup
1 pkg	OETKER Vanilla Sugar	1 pkg.
625 mL	milk	2½ cups
250 mL	sweet (unsalted) butter	1 cup
30 mL	cognac or brandy	2 tbsp.
375 mL	grated roasted nuts	1½ cups

Method:

COMBINE pudding and pie filling, sugar, vanilla sugar and 125 mL (½ cup) milk. Stir until smoothly blended.
RINSE saucepan with cold water.
HEAT remaining 500 mL (2 cups) milk to boiling. Stir in pudding mixture. Bring to boil again, stirring constantly.
REMOVE from heat. Cool to room temperature, stirring occasionally.
CREAM butter and cognac. Beat in pudding 15 mL (1 tbsp.) at a time. (Butter and pudding must be at same temperature to prevent curdling.) Gradually stir in nuts.

Wine Cream Filling

(Weincreme)

Ingredients:

1 pkg	OETKER Vanilla Pudding and Pie Filling	1 pkg.
175 mL	sugar	¾ cup
625 mL	white wine	2½ cups
250 mL	sweet (unsalted) butter	1 cup

Method:

COMBINE pudding and pie filling, sugar and 125 mL (½ cup) wine.

HEAT remaining wine to boiling. Stir in pudding mixture. Bring to boil again, stirring constantly.

REMOVE from heat. Cool to room temperature, stirring occasionally.

CREAM butter. Beat in pudding 15 mL(1 tbsp) at a time. (Butter and pudding must be at same temperature to prevent curdling.)

Chestnut Cream I

(Kastaniencreme I)

Ingredients:

1 kg	chestnuts	2 lb.
250 mL	milk	1 cup
250 mL	sugar	1 cup
1 pkg	OETKER Vanilla Sugar	1 pkg.
2 btl	OETKER Rum Essence	2 btl.
	or	
30 mL	rum	2 tbsp.
125 mL	whipping cream	½ cup

Method:

WASH chestnuts. Cut a small cross in skin. Roast on baking sheet. Remove skin. Simmer in milk until soft.

PRESS through sieve or food mill to make a smooth paste.

MIX chestnut puree, sugar, vanilla sugar and rum essence,

BEAT cream to stiff peaks. Fold into chestnut mixture.

Chestnut Cream II

(Kastaniencreme II)

Ingredients:

1 kg	chestnuts	2 lb.
175 mL	sugar	¾ cup
1 pkg	OETKER Vanilla Sugar	1 pkg.
2 btl	OETKER Rum Essence	2 btl.
	or	
30-45 mL	rum	2-3 tbsp.
250 mL	sweet (unsalted) butter	1 cup
3-4 sq	semi-sweet chocolate, melted and cooled	3-4 sq.

Method:

WASH chestnuts. Boil in water. Drain and peel. Press through sieve or food mill to make a smooth paste.

MIX chestnut puree, sugar, vanilla sugar and rum essence.

CREAM butter. Beat in puree and chocolate 15 mL (1 tbsp.) at a time. (Butter, puree and chocolate must be at same temperature to prevent curdling.)

Almond Cream

(Mandelcreme)

Ingredients:

1 pkg	OETKER Almond Pudding and Pie Filling	1 pkg.
250 mL	sugar	1 cup
625 mL	milk	2½ cups
30 mL	cognac or brandy	2 tbsp.
250 mL	sweet (unsalted) butter	1 cup
250 mL	unblanched almonds, ground	1 cup

Method:

COMBINE pudding and pie filling, sugar and 125 mL (½ cup) milk. Stir until smoothly blended.
RINSE saucepan with cold water.
HEAT remaining 500 mL (2 cups) milk to boiling. Stir in pudding mixture. Bring to boil again, stirring constantly.
REMOVE from heat. Stir in cognac. Cool to room temperature, stirring occasionally.
CREAM butter. Beat in pudding 15 mL(1 tbsp) at a time. (Butter and pudding must be at same temperature to prevent curdling.)
STIR in almonds.

NOTE: Pudding can be cooked easily in microwave.

Caramel Cream

(Karamelcreme)

Ingredients:

1 pkg	OETKER Caramel Pudding and Pie Filling	1 pkg.
250 mL	sugar	1 cup
625 mL	milk	2½ cups
250 mL	sweet (unsalted) butter	1 cup

Method:

PREPARE Caramel Cream the same as Almond Cream. Omit cognac and almonds.

Fruit Cream (Lemon, Orange, Raspberry, etc.)

(Fruchtcreme)

Ingredients:

1 pkg	OETKER Vanilla Pudding and Pie Filling	1 pkg.
50 mL	sugar	¼ cup
625 mL	fruit juice*	2½ cups
250 mL	sweet (unsalted) butter	1 cup

*If using fresh or frozen fruit, press through strainer to make juice.

Method:

COMBINE pudding and pie filling, sugar and 125 mL (½ cup) fruit juice.
HEAT remaining 500 mL (2 cups) juice to boiling. Stir in pudding mixture. Bring to boil again stirring constantly.
REMOVE from heat. Cool to room temperature, stirring occasionally.
CREAM butter. Beat in pudding 15 mL(1 tbsp) at a time. (Butter and pudding must be at same temperature to prevent curdling.)

Coffee or Lemon Glaze

(Kaffee bzw. Zitronenglasur)

Ingredients:

425 mL	sifted icing sugar	1¾ cups
45-60 mL	liquid (water, strong coffee or lemon juice)	3-4 tbsp.

Method:
STIR liquid into icing sugar, using just enough to make a smooth paste-like consistency.
VARIATION: Use these basic proportions of icing sugar to liquid to make any flavoured glaze. Use water or milk, coffee, lemon, raspberry, strawberry, orange or pineapple juice. Spirits (such as cherry brandy, cognac, rum, raspberry brandy, peach brandy, orange liqueur, etc.) can also be added as all or part of the liquid.

Cocoa Glaze

(Kakaoglasur)

Ingredients:

45 mL	butter or margarine	3 tbsp.
45-60 mL	hot water	3-4 tbsp.
425 mL	icing sugar	1¾ cups
75 mL	cocoa	⅓ cup

Method:
COMBINE butter and hot water in top of double boiler or a bowl. Place over boiling water to melt butter.
SIFT icing sugar and cocoa together into butter mixture. Stir to make a smooth paste-like consistency. Leave bowl over hot water to keep it soft for using.
STORE leftover glaze in a covered jar in refrigerator. Reheat as above to soften.

Fine Chocolate Glaze I

(Feine Schokoladeglasur)

Ingredients:

3-4 sq	semi-sweet chocolate	3-4 sq.
125 mL	whipping cream	½ cup

Method:
COMBINE chocolate and whipping cream in small saucepan. Bring to boil, stirring constantly. Cool slightly before using.

Chocolate Glaze II

(Schokoladeglasur)

Ingredients:

6-7 sq	semi-sweet chocolate	6-7 sq.
125 mL	sweet (unsalted) butter	½ cup

Method:
COMBINE chocolate and butter in top of double boiler. Place over boiling water until mixture melts. Stir well to make a smooth paste.

Egg White Glaze

(Eiweissglasur)

Ingredients:

450 mL	sifted icing sugar	1¾ cups
1	egg white	1
	lemon juice	

Method:
COMBINE icing sugar and egg white in mixing bowl. Stir in just enough lemon juice to make a paste-like consistency.

Caramel Glaze

(Karamelglasur)

Ingredients:

250 mL	fine granulated sugar or fruit sugar	1 cup
125 mL	sweet (unsalted) butter	½ cup

Method:
HEAT sugar in a heavy metal pan to a golden colour.
ADD butter. Bring to a boil once. Stir to a smooth glaze. Use immediately as glaze thickens and hardens very quickly.

Recipe Index